THE SHIFTING FOUNDATIONS OF MODERN NATION-STATES: REALIGNMENTS OF BELONGING

Nation-states today are under pressure from many directions. In western Europe, for example, they are being challenged by the call of assimilation into a larger supra-national polity. Elsewhere, as in central and southeastern Europe, nation-states are being challenged internally by separatist forces demanding independence or self-determination for particular ethnic groups. In either instance, the ultimate aim is not so much a breaking of bonds but rather a realignment of belonging.

When the prospect of prosperity and the good life requires an adjustment of national identities and alliances, national myths are mobilized in the effort. Personal affiliations are often flexible and pragmatic. Some people will never renounce their original 'nation,' while others gladly assume two or three national identities in a lifetime, all with a deeply felt commitment. *The Shifting Foundations of Modern Nation-States* gathers together a distinguished, multidisciplinary group of authors to discuss concepts of national identity, focusing on examples of national myths from Europe, North America, and Asia. Presenting analysis of conditions and problems in various nations, the essays in the volume raise important historical and theoretical issues, thus creating new space for thinking about questions of nationhood.

SIMA GODFREY is the director of the Institute for European Studies at the University of British Columbia.

FRANK UNGER is a professor with the Institute for European Studies at the University of British Columbia.

The Green College Thematic Lecture Series provides leading-edge theory and research in new fields of interdisciplinary scholarship. Based on a lecture program and conferences held at Green College, University of British Columbia, each book brings together scholars from several disciplines to achieve a new synthesis in knowledge around an important theme. The series provides a unique opportunity for collaboration between outstanding Canadian scholars and their counterparts internationally, as they grapple with the most important issues facing the world today.

The Green College Thematic Lecture Series

The Shifting Foundations of Modern Nation-States: Realignments of Belonging

Edited by Sima Godfrey and Frank Unger

UNIVERSITY OF TORONTO PRESS
Toronto Buffalo London

© University of Toronto Press Incorporated 2004
Toronto Buffalo London
Printed in Canada

ISBN 0-8020-3501-9 (cloth)
ISBN 0-8020-8394-3 (paper)

Printed on acid-free paper

National Library of Canada Cataloguing in Publication

The shifting foundations of modern nation-states: realignments
of belonging / edited by Sima Godfrey and Frank Unger.

(Green College thematic lecture series)
ISBN 0-8020-3501-9 (bound).   ISBN 0-8020-8394-3 (pbk.)

1. National state.   2. National state – History.   I. Godfrey, Sima
II. Unger, Frank   III. Series.

JC311.R42 2004   320.1   C2003-905745-3

University of Toronto Press acknowledges the financial assistance to
its publishing program of the Canada Council for the Arts and the
Ontario Arts Council.

University of Toronto Press acknowledges the financial support for
its publishing activities of the Government of Canada through the
Book Publishing Industry Development Program (BPIDP).

Contents

THE SHIFTING FOUNDATIONS OF
MODERN NATION-STATES

Introduction

SIMA GODFREY AND FRANK UNGER

Nation-states today are under pressure from opposite directions. In some parts of the world – for example, in Western Europe – they are being challenged by the movement towards assimilation into a larger, supra-national polity. Supporters of integration argue that, aside from the obvious benefits in the matter of peace and security, the new global economic order has rendered politics based on the traditional nation state outmoded and somehow insufficient for the modern political-economic environment. They want to overcome the nation-state by extending it.

In contrast, in other parts of the world – for example, in central and southeastern Europe – some former nation-states have been success-fully challenged from within by separatist forces demanding 'indepen-dence' or 'national self-determination' for particular ethnic groups. These groups have argued that their interests have been violated and their freedom suppressed by a federal government. They want to over-come the nation-state by breaking it up.

On closer inspection, however, these opposing challenges often re-veal themselves as two sides of the same coin. Since its founding in April 1951 with the Treaty of Paris (as the European Coal and Steel Community), the European Community has ridden a wave of astonish-ing prosperity and continuous expansion. After the collapse of Soviet-dominated socialism in eastern Europe, the newly named European Union assumed not only the image of unshakeable political and eco-nomic stability, but also something like the role of the last remaining counterweight to the hegemony of the shareholder-driven capitalism relentlessly pushed by the last remaining military superpower, the United States. Notwithstanding its often noted democratic deficits, the

EU is now generally seen as the best example of a transnational political organization that really works. This is placing pressure on individual nation-states in all of Europe.[1] Depending on the circumstances, this pressure expresses itself in different ways. If a significant number of people in the nations that make up the present EU are prepared to concede some of their home nations' sovereignty, they obviously do not sense a great loss, since they expect to be more than compensated by the gains that come with belonging to the greater union.[2] And if groups in formerly quite legitimate European nations outside the EU – for example, in the Balkans – desire to abandon their former nation and demand secession in the name of their 'ethnic' units, it may actually amount to the same thing. In many cases these fiercely nationalist 'secessionists' are actually seeking independence as a means of improving their chances of gaining access to the EU, especially when the multiethnic nation they are trying to leave is still associated with socialism and anti-Western policies. That is to say, the ultimate aim is not so much the breaking of bonds, but rather a realignment of belonging. This phenomenon can be observed in the United Kingdom, where Scottish and Welsh 'nationalists' wholeheartedly embrace the EU, in large part because it will allow them to emancipate themselves from their intra-national hegemon, England.

If the prospect of prosperity and the good life requires an adjustment of national identities or alliances, so be it. And if there are old myths and ancient tales available that can be used for the severing of bonds with the present community, so much the better. Those myths and tales can easily be forgotten again and assigned to collective oblivion, should the new community and the obligations of their *acquis communautaire* demand it. Until this happens, however, fierce nationalism may reign supreme, providing ample material for penetrating reflections about the astonishing 'renationalization' of eastern European politics after the demise of socialism.[3]

Anthony D. Smith, arguably the leading theoretician of nationalism in the English-speaking world, distinguishes four competing paradigms for explaining the nature, power, and incidence of nations and nationalism: the primordialist, the perennialist, the modernist, and the ethno-symbolic.[4] Smith makes a strong argument for his own approach, the ethno-symbolic one, which represents a kind of synthesis of the other three paradigms; however, he is not entirely persuasive in his criticism of the modernist approach. Modernists see nations and nationalism essentially as products of the processes of modernization, with the

French Revolution as the defining moment 'when nationalism was introduced into the movement of world history' as a political ideology.[5] Whatever individual examples of allegedly older 'nations' may be cited in order to challenge this view, they do not add up to a convincing criticism of the fundamental insight represented by the modernist paradigm: that nations are practical constructions, not inherited archetypes. 'Like the goods produced in the age of industry and nationalism, all national ideas are artificial,' writes Panikos Panayi.[6] Political leaders may see the idea of an ancient bond in order to arouse passion, and occasionally they may even 'evoke the moral imperative of dying for [that bond],' but in order to have its effect that bond always needs to be connected to a collective vision. Invocations of primordial origins inspire a people to communal action only when those invocations are at the same time associated with the promise of a brigher future for the present-day community. This brighter future may be an illusion, or it may be a cynical misrepresentation by power-hungry leaders, but without something of its kind, calls for national 'brotherhood' will remain unheard. For example, Croatians, are commonly regarded as among the fiercest ethno-nationalists in Europe, yet many would freely admit that they strongly embraced their Croatian-ness (or their rabid anti-Serbism, to be precise) not in the least to improve their chances of being accepted later as legitimate stakeholders in 'the West' in general, and in the European Union in particular. A classical realignment of belonging happened before in Germany, a nation whose citizens were at one time notoriously chauvinistic. Seventy years ago, a great majority of Germans idolized a political leadership that set out to squash the rest of continental Europe under its 'racial' thumb and to have millions of people killed in the name and interests of an ethnically 'pure' nation state. Today, a solid majority of educated Germans under fifty regularly name the European Union as their first choice of identity. Right-wing chauvinism has not quite dried out in Germany, but it has little if any chance of becoming a hegemonic popular force.

Whatever position one takes in academic discussions about the 'phylogenetic' roots of nations and nationalism, it seems clear that people's choices of belonging are flexible and more often than not blatantly pragmatic. Some will never renounce their original 'nation,' whereas others gladly assume two or even more national identities in a lifetime, all of them with a deeply felt commitment.[7] Such a position does not amount to a flat assertion of cultural diffusionism or the debunking of a fundamental human institution; rather, it represents the empirical acknowledgment that it is the actions of human beings – defined by Max Weber as the practical pursuit of deliberate (albeit not necessarily 'rational') intentions – that determine the character and fate of societies and the movement of history. As such, it is the deliberate actions of human beings, not mysterious primordial forces, that make or break nations. With one important caveat: as Marx and Weber remind us, although humans pursue their actions at any given time with freedom of choice, they do so in a historical environment – an environment not of their own making but rather created by past generations.

Informed by this epistemological position, we asked some colleagues – historians, journalists, political scientists, and sociologists – to provide us with interdisciplinary accounts of the state of the particular nations on which they have been working for most of their careers. Since the plurality of nations implies diverse voices and distinct narratives, we selected these colleagues to ensure the representation of multiple discourses and registers on the theme of nationhood, rather than to offer a sustained conversation on any one point of contention. We invited them to come to the University of British Columbia and speak in a lecture series we called 'The Myths of Nations.' The series, as we conceived it, was to focus less on theoretical arguments about nations and nationalism than on the specific conditions and problems of the respective nations discussed. At the same time, we expected that broader historical and theoretical questions would arise from these specific cases, thus creating a new space for thinking about questions of nationhood.

It should be admitted here that the final choice of the nations to be included in this book does not precisely match the original lecture series and is the result of opportunity as much as deliberate choice. The main criterion was the quality of the contributors and the character of the contributions, not the 'importance' of a country; however, we hope the sample of nations presented in this volume will contribute as much to theoretical discussions of modern nations and nationalism as would a more deliberately 'theoretical' treatment of the subject matter. We hope the articles in this volume will prove valuable both to students of area studies and to scholars of nations and nationalism.

Ramsay Cook opens the volume with his essay 'Canada: A Post-Nationalist Nation?' Canada represents the telling case of a nation-state that is being challenged from two directions. Some Canadians would support a political and economic union with their great neighbour to the south; others continue to advocate political independence for parts of the nation (i.e., Quebec or the Western provinces). Again, a mechanism similar to the one observed in Europe seems to be at work here: on closer inspection, both assaults on the Canadian nation-state seem to be motivated in equal parts by a desire for independence and by a search for a new community in which regional interests might be better served than under the auspices of the old nation.

Cook begins his essay by distinguishing between 'ethnic nations' and 'civic nations,' the first based on alleged bloodlines, the second on citizenship and territory. He then provides an overview of the history of nationalism and nationalisms in Canada, a 'civic nation' *par excellence*. He reminds us that even this classical civic nation has witnessed attempts to sell her as something more than that, by appealing to a supposed 'northern-ness' as the defining feature of Canadians. Other Canadians have seen this as little more than a sublime version of Anglo-Saxonism, and French-Canadian separatism was inspired by this as much as by Catholic corporatist antimodernism, which was commonly viewed as its original source.

According to Cook, the Quebec question will stay with us, even though recent polls show a decline in the support for sovereignty. But then the long-held assumption that Canada is a bicultural country has become obsolete. Outside as well as inside Quebec, multiculturalism has become a fact of life. In this multicultural Canada, the First Nations have now assumed a distinct political role for themselves. Cook reminds us that by voting nearly unanimously against Quebec independence in 1995, the James Bay Cree, and other First Nations voters, indicated their decisive support for the preservation of Canada's unity.

Cook presents this to us as an ironic comment on the strange ways of 'ethnic' nationalism. But then he also sees this conundrum precisely as an encouraging sign for the future of the Canadian nation. In Cook's view, it will certainly be a civic nation, one composed of many cultures that mutually accept one another. Borrowing the term from Benedict Anderson, Cook's project for the Canada of the future is an 'imagined community of real communities.'

Dietmar Schirmer also addresses the limits of ethnically determined myths of nations. He takes issue specifically with what he calls the 'master-narrative of German nationalism,' which he identifies as 'ethnocultural.' Germany is often regarded as the classic example of an ethnocultural understanding of national belonging based on an alleged blood relationship as opposed to the concept of the 'civic nation' based simply on citizenship and place of birth. Schirmer contends that this version of

German nationalism needs to be complemented by the concept of 'statism.'

Schirmer distinguishes three stages in the development of German nationalism. Early nationalism had as its objective the creation of a German nation-state out of nearly two thousand kingdoms, duchies, cities, and other minute units, which together formed the Holy Roman Empire of the German Nation. It was shaped by both the French Enlightenment and the later experience of Napoleonic imperial expansion, and it developed into an anti–foreign liberation nationalism that was, at the same time, antirevolutionary, because the imperial enemy was a revolutionary nation. It developed a claim for the general superiority of the German *Geist* over the 'mechanical rationality' of the French and the British, and German philosophers such as Schelling, Herder, Schiller, and Novalis attempted to establish a new mythology of Reason as a higher form of thought, culminating in the dialectic and learned philosophy of Hegel.

But this 'romantic' nationalism was soon to be joined by the uncompromising and sometimes quite cynical statism of one of the largest German states, Prussia. As a multiethnic political unit with no clear borders, it could not resort to an ethno-linguistic argument for the communality of its subjects. The Prussian masters thus resorted to a relentless glorification of the state, and its most famous ruler, Frederick II, declared himself the 'state's first servant' – a seemingly modest depiction that provided the legitimation for the most ruthless kind of absolutism. This tradition also created the particularly German institution of *Beamtentum*, which is most commonly translated as 'civil service' but is much more than that. In Prussia, as in the early years of the German Empire after 1871, this institution served as the organizing principle for the hierarchization of society, whereby an individual's status was the direct reflection of his or her proximity to the state and its institutions.

The 'statist' tradition of the civil servants survived and helped the country deal with two vastly different periods in its history. During the Weimar Republic, most Wilhelminian-appointed civil servants remained loyal to the new order, although they were by no means turning Republican in their way of thinking. And the same principle worked for the Nazis: a conservative civil service that perhaps loathed the upstart Hitler nevertheless displayed unswerving loyalty to the Nazi state until the very end.

In postwar West Germany this statist tradition was reaffirmed by the preservation of *Beamtentum*. Furthermore, the adherence to *ius sanguinis* as the basis for citizenship remained firmly entrenched, although it was employed less and less restrictively over the years. Not until 1999 was it modified, by a new citizenship law that for the first time since 1913 made German citizenship an entitlement for certain groups of people and individuals who were born in Germany but not of German parents. But this took place after the Maastricht Treaty had already established a European citizenship.

Like Schirmer, Marta Petrusewicz re-examines regional contingencies in the formation of a modern nation state's early history – in this instance, Italy. As was the case with Prussia and Germany, so Piedmont-Sardinia became the driving force behind Italian unification, with the Sardinian king, Victor Emanuel II, becoming King of Italy. Petrusewicz explains how the Italian path to unification under the leadership of Piedmont-Sardinia not only defined what was going to be 'Italy' but also succeeded in discrediting and disadvantaging the southern part of the nation, the Mezzogiorno, virtually until the present day. For much of northern Italy, the South represents 'Africa' rather than 'Europe,' 'passion' rather than 'reason,' 'peasant culture' rather than 'industry,' and the raw unpredictability of Vesuvius rather than the measured grandeur of civic architecture.

Petrusewicz sets out to demonstrate that there is little in the South's concrete historical past that would justify this stereotype, except for a ruthless campaign carried out by the Neapolitan feudal rulers to crush the liberal revolution of 1848, which was – at least in Naples – as sophisticated and enlightened as any movement in contemporary Paris, Vienna, or Berlin. During the entire first half of the nineteenth century, Naples had been a beehive of liberalism; students, liberals, and other progressive-minded people flocked there from all parts of the country to participate in its exciting ways. At the time, progressive southerners saw their area as perhaps not quite on the level of Britain, France, or Prussia, but certainly ahead of Russia – and with the potential to catch up with the best. In other words, the South was seen as a 'quasi-nation' and southerners certainly acted as if it was. When the king crushed the revolution of 1848, the intellectuals hoped the people would rise up; not only did they not do so, but in some dramatic instances they actually joined forces with the oppressor. Petrusewicz contends that this disappointing behaviour by the masses at the time of the counterrevolution led (southern) Italian intellectuals to disdain southern 'backwardness.' The southern *popolo* became *volgo*, and the South became the 'problem' as well as an alleged drain on national resources. To this day, it has remained so in the eyes of northerners.

Following Petrusewicz's reflections on Italy, Frank Unger turns to the United States. He takes a somewhat iconoclastic look at that country, whose recent political behaviour in the international arena has caused some concern and irritation even among its closest allies.

Unger re-examines the making of the American Constitution in light of its historical circumstances, and he questions the widely accepted belief in the enlightened and democratic character of the United States at its inception and ever since. Drawing on the writings of Sacvan Bercovich, Unger examines in particular the role of rhetoric in social cohesion. Here, he picks up on the old question first posed by the German historian Werner Sombart. 'Why is there no socialism in the United States?' In this context, he takes a fresh look at Frederick Jackson Turner's frontier thesis, which has served as an explanation, and concludes that the frontier alone would not have been a sufficient condition, because other countries had a similar frontier without the same effect (Canada, Australia). Instead, the explanation he offers is that the propertied classes in the United States succeeded in establishing a laissez-faire capitalist system by planting the emotional and rhetorical buttresses of religious conviction and utopian sanguinity. This stabilizing sleight of hand succeeded beyond the dreams of the European propertied classes, who had long had to put up with antagonizing class politics from two directions – those of the old feudal interests, and those of the political organizations of the new working classes. But this erstwhile blessing is indeed mixed. For it suggests somewhat disturbingly that the United States is now the only country in the world whose political culture is firmly rooted in the assumption that it has little to learn from anyone abroad: all answers must come from within. In the modern world, which is increasingly interconnected and politically egalitarian, such a posture is unsustainable, and not just in political terms.

Friends and allies who have come to feel aggravated by the virtual solipsism of American political behaviour often attribute their irritation to the 'unilateralism' of the present government of George W. Bush. However, Unger contends that solipsism and the belief in the exceptional role and status of 'America' are not confined to any particular government; rather, they function as structural elements of the American political tradition, sometimes more, sometimes less pronounced.

Looking at a very different republican tradition, Thomas Ferenczi, an editor with the distinguished French daily *Le Monde*, takes issue with what he sees as the French myth of 'the Republic.' He draws on the distinction made by Régis Debray for whom the French idea of the *republic* is defined in opposition to and as a deliberate counter-concept to the American idea of *democracy*. American democracy is associated with federalism and the rule of law; in contrast, French republicanism is associated with unity and the sovereignty of the people – themes that inform and shape the imagination and education of every child raised in France. And whereas in the American democracy every John or Jane can become president (if he or she has the money to run an election campaign), French republicans take pride in their unifying system of education, which filters out the best and the brightest for the upper echelons of French politics.

Ferenczi contends that republicanism in its radical ideological form is detrimental to the increasingly multiethnic French people, and he recommends that the French embrace some aspects of the American idea of democracy. He sees the tradition of the virtuous Jacobin Republic – commonly evoked by French proponents of the republic – as an outdated myth; furthermore, when that myth is harnessed to foster popular resentment against the United States and the European Union (and, one might add here, the forces of market globalism), its impact is negative.

Ferenczi provides a new spin to the long debate between two opposing traditions of modern politics that have coexisted since the French and American revolutions. The debate opened more than two hundred years ago, when Federalists and Anti-Federalists argued over the constitution of the newly independent American republic. However, it was French political thinkers who first summarized these opposing philosophies in a coherent fashion. They were most succinctly expressed in Montesquieu's and Rousseau's views of the ultimate objective of the 'good state.' According to Montesquieu, the state was to help carry out the empirical *volonté de tous*; according to Rousseau, it was to implement an ideal *volonté générale*. Ferenczi sides with the *volonté de tous*, because nobody can legitimately claim to know the *volonté générale*, and therefore its objectives can only be decreed by an elite whose motives may not be entirely unselfish. French republicans may or may not heed his suggestion, and they may also point out that Ferenczi fails to consider the counterveiling danger of a class-structured civil society in which a skilful ruling class can manipulate the *volonté de tous* in its own selfish interests without ever having to violate the rules of democracy.

To the east of France, in the somewhat confusing and confused world of postcommunism, questions of the nation and of nationalism have shifted from the ideological periphery to the centre of attention. Andreas Heinemann-Grüder considers the case of Russia, which until very recently was the leading power and symbol of 'socialist internationalism' and to this day is the largest country in the world. Since the dissolution of the Soviet Union – brought about in large part by internal Russian politics – the country has been searching for a new national identity to replace and at the same time perpetuate the 'national' narrative of the Soviet Union, which was once generally regarded as the second most powerful nation on earth.

Heinemann-Grüder takes a close look at the domestic debates over what actually defines Russian national 'identity.' He then asks the following four questions:

1 What do national myths contribute to social cohesion?
2 What explains the sequence of present-day national myths in Russia?
3 How are national self-images related to public self-perceptions – that is, how do elite-produced narratives connect with the commonsense thinking of the people?
4 Why are there a host of competing national images instead of just a single hegemonic one – as, for example, in the United States?

In Russia, as in all other 'transformation countries' in Eastern Europe, the collapse of the socialist system and the breakdown of state repression resulted in a great deal of economic hardship for most of the population. The social safety net broke down, and so did the welfare state in general, including the health care system. These hardships of transformation discredited Western liberalism in the eyes of many people; they also fostered a strong yearning for a return to the old socialist system under the guise of chauvinist nationalism. The former communist concept of popular sovereignty was translated into the 'modern' concept of ethnic sovereignty. In other words, the concept of 'people's power' was successfully turned against its (communist) originators while the socialist system was being destroyed, but it did not have enough steam to be used as the basis for building a postsocialist civil (bourgeois) society, or, to be more precise, for constructing a new bourgeois society as a civil society. Heinemann-Grüder states, that in Russia, as in many other postsocialist states, we therefore 'have a fledgling bourgeois society without civility.'

Heinemann-Grüder then examines how in these confusing circumstances and with no hegemonic national idea, the various competing elites have tried desperately to revive old images of national identity – all of them already present in the nineteenth century – for the future purpose of giving some sort of meaning to the new Russia. He sifts out four types of national narratives as articulated by Russian proponents of national identities: Westernist, Eurasianist, Slavophile, and Statist. All four types, including the Eurasianist, define themselves vis-à-vis (western) Europe. For Russians, contends Heinemann-Grüder, Europe, not the United States, remains the defining *Other*, either as an ideal to strive for or as an object lesson in what to avoid.

Heinemann-Grüder concludes that there is no post-Soviet national model *sui generis* and that there will not be one in the foreseeable future. The good news is that so far there is almost no aggressive ethnocentric nationalism that could pose a serious threat to Russia's neighbours and the rest of the world. Russia 'seems stuck between dysfunctional, anachronistic role models and a still distant idea of a community of citizens based on positive identification with the constitutional order and the political system.' In order to really get back on track, Heinemann-Grüder argues, Russia needs efficiency of governance and civic legitimacy, rather than attempts at repeating the nation-building classes it flunked in the nineteenth century.

Following Heinemann-Grüder, Laszlo Kontler discusses the case of Hungary. Hungary has always played a special role in the history of socialism in Eastern Europe. Though a member of the Warsaw Pact, its people had never embraced Soviet-induced postwar political-economic changes, and it led the way in challenging that system. In 1956 the Hungarian uprising – by far the most serious and violent challenge to be faced by any socialist regime before 1989 – provoked a massive intervention by the Red Army. This in turn led to the first significant change in postwar socialist policies: the de-emphasizing of the Stalinist model of heroic productionism, and its replacement, under new Prime Minister Janos Kadar, by a more consumer-oriented economic policy appropriately nicknamed 'Goulash Communism.' Later still, Hungary led the way in introducing market mechanisms to the planned economy. In 1973 it even joined GATT. By that point it was seen by many Soviet economists, who were pondering the stagnation of the Soviet economy, as a possible example for other socialist countries. In the summer of 1989 it was the Hungarian socialist government that brought about the final collapse of the Cold War system in Europe by unilaterally opening its border with Austria; this allowed thousands of East Germans to leave the hitherto fenced-in territory of the Eastern Bloc for the greener pastures of West Germany. This in turn brought about the terminal crisis of the German Democratic Republic, which led to the breaking of the Berlin Wall in 1989 and to formal German unification in 1990.

Since 1990, Hungarians have been struggling over the symbolic uses of their past. Kontler takes issue with his compatriots over the disturbing fact that most postcommunist Hungarians have apparently chosen 20 August (1083) – the day of the final laying to rest of Stephen I, the founder of the Hungarian monarchy – as their day of collective commemoration, instead of 15 March (1848), the day of the (ultimately failed) national bourgeois revolution under Lajos Kossuth. During the 1970s and 1980s, 15 March became the symbolic date for the (bourgeois) opposition movement against the socialist regime. When the regime stepped back in 1990 and new political parties could take part in free elections, the political identification of Hungarians took an ominous shift. Since then, well over 50 per cent of Hungarians have named 20 August as the 'holy day' that should define the identity of postcommunist Hungary.

Kontler does not list all the reasons why Hungarians, remarkably, prefer an ancient feudal king rather than a liberal-bourgeois revolutionary as the symbol for the identity of a nation freshly 'liberated' from a socialist regime. That said, this choice indicates that the symbolism of 1848, the year of the modern bourgeois revolution, does not appeal to most present-day Hungarians – at least not exclusively. They seem to prefer a more vague, imprecise symbolism, as if they prefer to leave open the option of which elements of liberalism and socialism they wish to finally amalgamate into their idea of a modern Hungary.

Benedict Anderson closes the volume with his account of the condition of Indonesia after the fall of the Suharto regime. He was finally allowed to visit that country after being declared *persona non grata* there for more than twenty years. Most people know Anderson as a seminal theoretician of nationalism and the author of *Imagined Communities*. But this is something of a misinterpretation. Anderson of course knows that he has contributed significantly to our theoretical understanding of nations and nationalism, but he sees this as more of a spin-off from his main scholarly and – one needs to add here – political interest: the region of Southeast Asia, especially the archipelago called Indonesia.

Indonesia is one of the oldest regions of human habitation – the first remains of *Pithecanthropus* to be found were on the island of Java – but as a modern 'nation' it has existed for just over half a century. Anderson developed an interest in the young nation and its culture(s) early on as a scholar, and he also participated in the post-colonial political struggles that culminated in the slaughter of half a million alleged and real communists by the American-backed Suharto forces in 1965. For Anderson, scholarly objectivity does not imply political impartiality but rather political involvement, because the pursuit of truth cannot be separated from the pursuit of justice. In this practical context, and with a clear political purpose in mind, Anderson developed his 'modernist' theories about nations and nationalism. It is not despite but precisely as a result of this association that his theoretical work gains its authenticity.

The most important lesson to learn from Anderson is that nationalism is not necessarily a bad thing if it comes in the form of patriotism. But what is patriotism? The great Viennese actor/comedian Helmut Qualtinger once defined a patriot as 'someone who is capable of being ashamed by his country.' Anderson picks up on precisely the same sentiment in the conclusion to his essay on Indonesia with an appeal to his readers:

> We pay taxes in long-term public investments of a hundred kinds – schools, universities, museums, highways, and so on – out of which we, as mortal individuals, will perhaps receive only minor and fleeting benefits. And we are able to feel ashamed of our nation's bad behaviour and the sometimes criminal practices of our nation's rulers, exactly because we have a future to which we feel accountable. It was this shame that drove frail and elderly Americans into the streets to protest against the savage idiocy of the American state's onslaught in Indochina. It is the same shame that drives comfortably-off Indonesian lawyers to devote themselves to helping the victims of the Indonesian military's brutal rapacity. They want a better future for their country. Don't we all?

In conclusion, it would seem that our yearning for belonging that finds its expression in the pervasive myths of nations could be put to better use if we consciously realized our common desires for the future instead of indulging in musings about an allegedly shared heroic past.

NOTES

1 An eminent scholar of European integration, Alan Milward, has argued, to the contrary, that the whole project of European integration was initiated

for the purpose of 'saving the European nation state.' This may well have been the case in the immediate postwar era, but some fifty years later, those original intentions have produced rather different results. See Alan Milward, *The European Rescue of the Nation State* (London: Routledge, 1992).

2 We are referring here to mainstream thinking within the EU countries. There is, of course, substantial scepticism and often passionate opposition to what is polemically called a transnational 'super-state' in almost every EU country; this is most pronounced in the English part of the United Kingdom and in some Scandinavian member states.

3 See for example Michael Ignatieff, *Blood and Belonging: Journeys into the New Nationalism* (Toronto: Viking, 1993).

4 Anthony D. Smith, *Myths and Memories of the Nation* (Oxford: Oxford University Press, 1999), 3.

5 Ibid., 6.

6 Panikos Panayi, *An Ethnic History of Europe since 1945* (Harlow, U.K.: Longman, 2000), 6.

7 Max Weber, another uncompromising representative of the 'modernist' understanding of nations, has pointed out the 'intimate connection of prestige-interests with the idea of the nation.' Max Weber, *Wirtschaft und Gesellschaft*, Studienausgabe Band II (Cologne: Kiepenheuer & Witsch, 1964), 677.

Canada: A Post-Nationalist Nation?

RAMSAY COOK

The best thing about Canada is that it is not this. It is this and that.

George Bowering

Over the past twenty years, the academic study of nationalism – to say nothing of the phenomenon itself – has grown at an astounding pace. Where once it was merely a subject for the detailed historical analysis of particular communities or ethnic groups, nationalism has recently become a subject approached from a multiplicity of perspectives: history, sociology, literature, religion, political science, and anthropology. Moreover, new theoretical prescriptions abound as class, race, gender, and ethnicity expand their explanatory empires. To his recent survey *Nationalism and Modernism*, which assesses work published since his first survey *Theories of Nationalism* in 1971, Anthony Smith has appended a bibliography of twenty closely printed pages of mostly new work.[1] Much of the intellectual excitement in this exploding field turns on the controversy over whether nations are born, and therefore ancient, or made and thus modern. In its postmodern form, the question is whether nations are real – essential – or imagined – contingent. Is the study of nationalism, Smith asked in the first issue of the new journal, *Nations and Nationalism*, 'gastronomy or geology'?[2]

That there should be controversy over the nature and definition of 'nation' and 'nationalism' is hardly surprising, especially in Canada, where the subject has been the main course at political and academic banquets for forty years, fifty years, a century, or more. At one level, of course, the question is easily answered. In juridical terms, the number of sovereign nations in the world can be established by consulting the membership lists of the United Nations. But that is too simple: it ignores the question of what gives some groups – say, Canadians – the right to membership – and what refuses that right to other groups – say, Scots or Turkish Kurds. Here, then, is the heart of the issue.

It has long been understood – and I would argue that modern scholarship has added little if anything to this understanding – that there are two general constructions of the term *nation*, both in use by the end of the eighteenth century. The first definition took the state as its frame of reference, its citizens forming the nation. In its modern form this definition is often called *republican* or *civic* because of its connection with the French Revolution – although it precedes that event, as Liah Greenfeld's dense work demonstrates.[3] There are many claimants to the authorship of this definition of nation: John Stuart Mill, who wrote of 'a feeling of common interest among those who live under the same government or are contained within the same natural or historical boundaries'; Ernest Renan, who emphasized consent, the nation as 'a daily plebiscite' based on 'shared glories in the past, a shared will in the present'; and Lord Acton, whose essay 'Nationality' argued that since the promotion of liberty was the chief end of the state, ethnic diversity was the best test and guarantee of that liberty. Acton's uniqueness – what distinguished him from other nineteenth-century liberals, including Mill and Renan – was his contention that a nationalism that identified one ethnic group with the state was a homogenizing force that aimed at the erasure of all other culturally distinct groups. Acton came very close to arguing that a nation is best defined – we might say imagined – as a set of civic values held in common by culturally diverse citizens; indeed, he claimed that civic values and ethnic diversity were inseparable. ('a state which does not include them [diverse ethnic groups] is destitute of the chief basis of self-government').[4]

Each of these definitions, and especially that of Acton, stands in direct opposition to the second notion of nation, which was formulated in reaction to the rationalism of the civic definition. The most explicit author of the ethno-linguistic conception of nation was, of course, the German philosopher J.G. Herder. Here are two passages in which he set out his essential position. First, on language: 'Without a common native tongue in which all classes are raised like branches on one tree there can be no true mutual understanding, no common patriotic development, no intimate common sympathy, no patriotic public.' And beyond language, Herder maintained that 'the most natural state is *one* national state with one national character. This it retains for ages, and this is most naturally formed when it is the object of its native princes; for nationality is as much a plant of nature as a family, only with more branches. Nothing therefore appears so indirectly opposite to the end of government than the unnatural enlargement of states, the wild mixing of all kinds of people and nationalities under one sceptre.'[5] Implicit in Herder's definition of nation is the so-called principle of national self-determination whereby culturally homogeneous nations have an absolute right to govern themselves. Whether such a right also belongs to culturally diverse nations seems never to have been tested, but for a country like Canada it is a question of considerable interest.

Although nations, both in the sense of nation-states and as culturally distinct groups (ethnie), existed well before the end of the eighteenth century,[6] nationalism as an ideology devised to legitimize the modern nation-state appeared in Europe during and in reaction to the French Revolution.[7] Nationalist ideology asserted that humanity was divided into distinct nations defined by language, culture, history, and social values, and perhaps religion, geography, and economic practices.[8] I would like to emphasize two points. The first is that nationalism is the ideology of a culturally homogeneous ethnic community, and might more accurately be called 'ethnonationalism,' which is Walker Connor's term.[9] Such homogeneity can be made out of historically disparate groups: peasants, as Eugene Weber has shown, can be made into Frenchmen.[10] The second point is that the focus of nationalist attention and loyalty is the ethnic nation, not the state or the country, although the aim is to make nation, state, and country coterminous. Loyalty directed toward a state or a country is distinct from nationalism and is more properly called patriotism. Early in *For the Love of Country*, his remarkable study of the language of nationalism, Maurizio Viroli writes: 'The language of patriotism has been used over the centuries to strengthen or invoke love of the political institutions and the way of life that sustain the common liberty of a people, that is, love of the republic; the language of nationalism was forged in late eighteenth century Europe to defend or reinforce the cultural, linguistic and ethnic oneness and homogeneity of a people.'[11]

It follows from these two contentions – the concept of ethno-nationalism and the distinction between patriotism and nationalism – that ethnic nations develop nationalism whereas civic nations cannot. Patriotism, on the other hand, is the necessary glue of civic communities. Eugen Weber has remarked: 'Where patriotism is about attachment, nationalism is about anxiety. And aggressiveness.'[12] Of course, these distinctions are imperfect, since most contemporary nations – at least in the democratic world – display both ethnic and civic traits. The trick for a country like Canada – and in an increasingly multicultural world, for many other nations – is to establish a workable balance, to imagine a community of communities that is real.

Let me now see if these distinctions and claims I have been making can contribute to an understanding of the various expressions of nationalism in Canada. In doing so I would like to use, with some reservations, the framework of 'imagined communities' as set out by Benedict Anderson. In his brilliant but often elusive book of that title, Anderson contends that 'a nation is an imagined political community – and imagined as both inherently limited and sovereign. It is imagined because even the members of the smallest nation will never know most of their fellow members, meet them, or even hear of them, yet in the minds of each lives the image of their community.' And he goes on to say that this community, no matter what the everyday realities of exploitation of one group by another, 'is always conceived as a deep horizontal relationship.'[13] Though Anderson doesn't say so, I think what he is describing here is the nation as it exists in the minds and aspirations of nationalists: a society in which collective values trump individual or group interests. Such societies rarely exist, which explains why nationalists are almost always critics of their own nations. That certainly is the message that can be drawn from the communities imagined by nationalists in Canada.

It is well known that the Fathers of Confederation were pragmatic lawyers for the most part, more given to fine tuning the details of a constitutional act than to waxing philosophical about human rights or national goals. Yet it is possible to glean from the Confederation debates a few features of their imagined community. Cartier talked about a 'new nationality' that would recognize both religious differences and ethnic plurality (French and English, Irish and Scots, Catholics and Protestants, he listed). There would be two languages in Quebec and in federal institutions. And the system would be federal, and not just because Lower Canadians, as Macdonald put it, 'being in a minority, with a different language, nationality and religion from the majority,' needed guarantees. Despite the existence of a common language and legal system in Upper Canada and the Maritimes, 'there was as great a disinclination on the part of the various Maritime Provinces to lose their individuality, as separate political organizations, as we observed in the case of Lower Canada itself.' So the 'new nationality' was a political nationality, not an ethnic one, not a homogeneous one.[14]

That might have seemed a good start, but it was not good enough for the young men who founded the Canada First movement in the years immediately after Confederation. They wanted something more bracing: a nationalism to inspire a new country mired in politics, patronage, and economic debates. Like many later nationalist intellectuals, they were vaguely aware that the new country lacked cultural unity (something they did not view as positive), so they appealed to the nation's supposed 'northern-ness.' 'A glance at the map of this continent, as well as the history of the past,' R.G. Haliburton declared in *The Man of the North*, 'will satisfy us that the peculiar characteristics of the new Dominion must ever be that it is a Northern country inhabited by the descendants of Northern races.' The persistence of this theme of the northern-ness of a people – almost all of whom live very near to the Canada-U.S. boundary – is demonstrated by its reappearance in John Ralston Saul's overly ambitious attempt to reimagine Canada in *Reflections of a Siamese Twin*. That the 'north,' or at least the exploitation of northern resources, has benefited southern Canada and drawn it closer to the United States, the major market, is an irony usually lost on the expositors of our 'northern' identity.[15]

After the collapse of the Canada First movement, some of its supporters moved on to other activities that revealed the essentially Anglo-Saxon ideology of their nationalism. Charles Mair denounced the idea that western Canada should be bilingual; George Denison proposed Imperial Federation, and Goldwin Smith called for the unification of the English-speaking peoples through annexation of Canada to the Great Republic to the south. This Anglo-Saxon ideology did much to limit French language rights outside Quebec before 1920, and to ensure Canada's participation in the Boer War and the Great War. Though much of the enthusiasm for the Empire declined after the Great War, that same Anglo-Saxon attitude underlay the newly dominant claim that Canada was a North American nation, with the implication that North America was English-speaking.[16]

This English-speaking imagined community had its counterpart in the French Canadian intellectual community. Since at least the 1830s, ethnic nationalism – sometimes diluted with liberalism – had been finding French-speaking proponents, notably Louis-Joseph Papineau. By the 1860s it had taken two forms: in its *rouge* guise, it rejected the idea of a new nationality as espoused by George-Étienne Cartier, claiming that French Canadians already were a nation and had no need for a new, potentially assimilating, one. The other form, which by the end of the nineteenth century had become dominant, was the clerical, conservative, integral ethnic nationalism often identified with the Ultramontaine Bishop Bourget of Montreal and the ultra-conservative journalist Jules-Paul Tardivel, the father of francophone separatism. Henri Bourassa had succeeded in combining French-Canadian patriotism with a conception of a dualistic Canada, but by the 1920s he had been pushed aside by the priest-historian Canon Lionel Groulx, whose reading of history led him to imagine French Canada gradually freeing itself from the scars of the conquest, liberalism, and capitalism and moving toward autonomous, Catholic, corporate bliss.[17]

These rival imagined communities never attracted large followings. Nevertheless, these ideologies, in diluted form, were not without influence. Certainly, by the 1930s, Quebec governments, especially the Union nationale, were presenting themselves as defenders of francophone culture and values. The volumes of the Report of the Tremblay Commission (1956) articulated exactly that position. In these same years the federal government in Ottawa was increasingly assuming the role of 'national' government, in response to a Canadian nationalism that was the result of the years of the Depression and the Second World War – a nationalism that French Canadians often suspected was really English-Canadian nationalism. While this was not entirely a founded suspicion – the Massey Commission, after all, included Father Georges-Henri Lévesque, and the CBC was paralleled by Radio-Canada – it was convincing enough that many French Canadians turned their attention to the construction of a more vigorous provincial/national state. In shorthand, that describes the Quiet Revolution of the 1960s, from which flowed the various separatist and quasi-separatist demands that state and nation be made to correspond in a new Quebec nation.[18] For these Quebeckers, the imagined community was no longer French Canada but rather Quebec.

In response to the challenge of Quebec nationalism, the heirs of Macdonald and Cartier began to construct a modified Canadian community, one that reinforced the original Confederation idea that each of the two cultures, French and English, could exist and even thrive within a single federal state. There were many variations on this central theme – bilingualism, biculturalism, different status for Quebec, and so on – but the important point is that there was a widespread recognition that the imagined community was in need of change. But just as it seemed that the age of bilingualism and biculturalism had come – the old French-Canadian dream of a compact of two nations – there was growing evidence that its time – at least the time of biculturalism – had in fact already passed. Many French Canadians continued to imagine a bicultural community; however, as Guy Laforest argues in *Trudeau et la fin d'un rêve canadien*,[19] something quite different had emerged in anglophone Canada and had begun to make its mark on the French-Canadian community as well. And that, of course, was multiculturalism, by which I mean the social fact, not the policy. And almost simultaneously, another voice was heard demanding recognition: the voice – or rather, voices – of Canada's native peoples.

Neither of these phenomena was new, only their intensity and the changed intellectual climate in which they were voiced. Let me look briefly at each in turn.

First, multiculturalism. As a social fact, multiculturalism has existed in Canada ever since foreign immigration began to people the country with a non-aboriginal population and certainly since the arrival of the Loyalists, themselves a mixed group of Iroquois, English, Germans, and Blacks. But it was not until the late nineteenth and early twentieth century that non-French/non-English immigrants began to arrive in sufficient numbers to challenge the traditional French-English dominance. The great waves of immigration that arrived in the Laurier years provoked the first great debate about multiculturalism. For the most part, though incompletely, the proponents of assimilation – Anglo-conformity, it is often called – carried the day. Both French and English Canadians were confident of the superiority of their cultures over those of the multitongued newcomers. But in the aftermath of the Second World War, English-speaking Canadians – though not French-speaking Canadians – were less certain that their culture should set the bar for full acceptance as 'Canadians.' As the number of immigrants multiplied, and so-called visible minorities joined more traditional newcomers, the issue became more complex. The power of this new 'third force' was first manifested in the terms of reference of the 1964 Royal Commission on Bilingualism and Biculturalism. That commission was initially designed to study the status of the two original 'founding peoples,' but it was quickly forced to add 'the other ethnic groups' to its agenda *and* membership. Two years after the key recommendation of that commission was implemented in the Official Languages Act of 1969, Parliament passed legislation recognizing and supporting 'multiculturalism.' From the outset, that action was almost as controversial as bilingualism, especially in Quebec, where nationalists then – and even now – viewed multiculturalism as a clever ploy designed to reduce the

French-Canadian presence in Canada to nothing more than that of another ethnic group. Many English Canadians, still devoted to the earlier assimilationist ideology, argued that official support for cultural pluralism would lead to the balkanization of the country. What many of them really feared, of course, was that the traditional cultural and political dominance of anglophones would be undermined.

The debate about multiculturalism is a continuing one, and at a sophisticated level turns on two general issues. The first concerns the relationship between the so-called founding peoples – English and French – and the newcomers. Can first comers have more rights, especially language rights, than second and third comers? Is it possible, in other words, for every individual to enjoy equal citizenship rights if some group rights are also recognized? Both Charles Taylor (somewhat reluctantly, I think) and Will Kymlicka (enthusiastically) have attempted to find positive solutions to this liberal dilemma. Kymlicka's contention that collective rights, which protect minority cultures from external infringements, are legitimate, whereas collective powers that enforce internal conformity are not, is a subtle one. So, too, is the distinction he draws between multinational and polyethnic societies, especially since he argues that Canada is both. For him, native people and French and English Canadians are national groups with national rights; other groups form a polyethnic population whose rights are cultural. The difference relates mainly though not entirely, to language rights. Polyethnicity within an English-language framework is a fair description of the Canada that is taking shape outside of Quebec.[20]

And what about Quebec? Having begun by vigorously opposing both the philosophical and the practical aspects of multiculturalism, many francophone Quebeckers have now come to accept a reality partially forced upon them by demography: the collapse of their birthrate and the requirements of their labour force. While denouncing federal multicultural policies, successive Quebec governments have adopted a program called 'interculturalism' that is barely distinguishable from the multicultural policies adopted by Ottawa and other Canadian provinces. Equally interesting, and perhaps more significant in the long run, is the growing evidence that despite Jacques Parizeau's famous outburst about 'money and ethnic votes' after the last referendum, many Quebec nationalists have gradually come to accept a definition of 'nation' that is inclusive. When in the summer of 1999 the nationalist daily Le Devoir asked a dozen intellectuals to write for a series titled 'Penser la nation québécoise,' only one, the philosopher

Serge Cantin, objected to the general view that traditional homogeneity had to be replaced by an acceptance of francophone polyethnicity. Cantin upheld the view of the late nationalist sociologist and guru, Fernand Dumont.[21] A more widely accepted view seems to be the one formulated by the historian Gérard Bouchard in *la nation québécoise au futur et au passé*. For Bouchard, the critical test of membership in the nation is the ability to live in French. In another place, Bouchard states: 'Je ne vois pas comment, si nous acceptons le fait que nos sociétés sont ouvertes à l'immigration sans discrimination donc à la diversité et à la différence, nous pourrions recréer une identité nationale ou collective qui fonctionne à l'homogénéité et à l'assimilation, comme jadis. C'est impossible. S'il faut respecter la diversité des croyances, les particularismes, alors, il faut reconstruire l'identité sur autres bases, sur des bases qui accommodent la pluralité ethnique.'[22] 'Nous sommes tous des pure-laine' was the way *Le Devoir* summed up its summer series. While that was too optimistic, even on the evidence of readers' response, it was not without some justification.

There is still a good deal that is problematic about the new pluralism, in both its French and English forms. The line between pluralism and assimilation is not always a clear one when French and English are the languages of citizenship. The commitment by contemporary Quebec nationalists to the idea of a territorial as opposed to an ethnic nation is obviously a move away from past exclusivism. But it is also obvious that any decision about the future of that territorial, polyethnic nation could be determined by the *pure-laine* francophones – the majority. This explains why in discussions of 'national history' in Quebec, by Gérard Bouchard and others, there is an obvious desire to use history to alter the 'imagined communities' of those for whom Quebec has not yet been accepted as a nation.[23] That same motivation can be discovered not very far below the surface in the proposals of anglophone advocates of 'national history.' That is especially evident in Jack Granatstein's controversial *Who Killed Canadian History?*, which concludes with this ringing call to historical arms: 'We have a nation to save and a future to build.'[24]

Let us now take a cursory look at the so-called 'national question' represented by the Native peoples – or, as their leaders prefer, 'the First Nations.' Almost simultaneous with its warm embrace of official multiculturalism, the Trudeau government proclaimed a new policy for Native people in a 1969 White Paper. That ill-fated statement called for the full integration of Native people into Canadian society through the gradual elimination of the special status implied in reservation policy and the paternalism of the Department of Indian Affairs. The outraged rejection of this proposal by Native leaders across the country led over the next decade to demands not for integration as individuals, but rather recognition of Native people's collective inherent rights accompanied by substantial land settlements. The First Nations intended to build their own imagined communities. In 1992 the Assembly of First Nations presented the fullest version of these claims in a radical constitutional document titled *To the Source*, which demanded quasi-sovereign constitutional powers, separate judicial institutions, exemption from the Canadian Charter of Rights and Freedoms, and official language status, among other things. The Charlottetown Accord of 1992 accepted almost all of these proposals.[25] These claims against Canada, the native leaders made plain, were equally made against the national territorial goals of Quebec. In the autumn of 1992, Grand Chief Ovide Mercredi underlined more clearly than anyone except Pierre Trudeau the full implications of competing national claims. First in a heated exchange before a committee of the Quebec National Assembly and then in *Le Devoir*, Mercredi asserted that 'if it belongs to Quebeckers and no one else to decide what powers to grant themselves [the claim made by both Quebec political parties], to ensure their full flowering, then it is the same for us.'[26] And the James Bay Cree, as a prelude to a five-hundred page legal brief against Quebec's claim to their territory, titled *Sovereign Injustice*, stated:

> We are *Eeyouch*. We are a people. We have our own land, *Eeyou Astchee*. We are an organized society of Aboriginal people forming part of the community of the world's indigenous peoples. We are the original inhabitants of our territory, and have occupied our land and governed ourselves for the past 9000 years.
>
> ...
>
> The myth persists in Quebec and elsewhere in Canada, that this country consists of two founding nations or peoples. This fiction constitutes a practical denial of our presence, our rights and status, and our role in the history, economy and well-being of this country.
>
> ...
>
> This is certain: The Crees will be here. We are not going anywhere. Nothing will be done with us, now or in the future, without our informed consent.[27]

In October 1995, in the Quebec Referendum, the *Cree*, together with all the other Native and Inuit communities, voted almost unanimously against the sovereignty option. Once again, as in 1990 when Elijah Harper's white eagle feather signalled the defeat of the Meech Lake Accord, the votes of Canada's first people proved critical to the slim majority that gave the country another chance.

That referendum has had a peculiar, numbing impact on all of Canada. It is as if, having drawn unexpectedly close to the abyss of self-destruction, no one wants to tread that path again. Though none of the questions that have agitated the country over the past four decades has been resolved, a strange and perhaps ominous silence, broken only occasionally by debates on the Nisga'a Treaty or the so-called Clarity Bill, hangs over them all. So let me conclude with some speculations about where we might be going, what sort of imagined community of communities might be in the making.

First, the Quebec question. The constant reappraisal and readjustment of relations between French and English Canadians, between a self-conscious minority and an often unsympathetic or at least uninterested majority, is central to our history. That means that the Quebec question will not go away – probably ever – and that the relationship will need constant reimagining. It will not go away because Quebec will not – barring disaster shocking to think of – separate even though the embers of nationalism will continue to glow, and even to burn brightly from time to time. Indeed it appears, as Lysianne Gagnon remarked in a recent comment on the fluctuating fate of the sovereignty option, that 'sovereignty is a 'dream that most people don't want to come true.' The intoxicating dream repeats itself, but so does the realism of the morning awakening. This rash prediction is based on more than the latest public opinion polls, which show a decline in support for sovereignty and a persistent distaste for another referendum.[28]

The changing demographic shape of Quebec's francophone population, the transforming social structure, and the obvious success of the language laws continue to subtlety undermine support for sovereignty. And note that even with those language laws, Quebec – especially Montreal – is easily among the most multilingual societies in North America.[29] Multicultural immigration and linguistic diversity have gradually undermined the traditional concept of ethnic nationalism, and that, in turn, will dilute the potency of the sovereignist appeal. This does not mean that Quebec will become just a passive province in the

Canadian federal system; rather, it means that as its society changes, so will the character of is demands for constitutional change. In Quebec, as elsewhere in the democratic world, a postnationalist phase is being born. The frustrations of long-established anglophone Quebeckers may be understandable, but it is certainly not time to say goodbye![30] Consider instead the proposition of a young Quebec historian, Jocelyn Létourneau, whose contribution to Le Devoir's 'Penser la nation québécoise' series insisted that 'Penser l'avenir du Québec sans prendre en compte la centralité du fait canadien dans l'identité québécoise, c'est comme penser l'avenir du Canada en négligeant la centralité du fait français dans l'identité canadienne.'[31]

Outside of Quebec, multiculturalism as a policy or policies remains a matter of debate. But multiculturalism as a social fact is exactly that: a fact. According to the recently released 2001 census, the foreign-born population has increased from 16.1 to 18.4 per cent since 1991; at present, the foreign-born population of Toronto is 43 per cent (perhaps the highest of any city in the world), Vancouver 37.5 per cent, and Montreal 18.4 per cent. In urban areas with large numbers of 'visible minorities' there is sometimes encountered an uneasy relationship that can burst into racist words and even actions. A recent book of essays titled Painting the Maple, marred as it sometimes is by the opaque and abstract language of contemporary cultural criticism, nevertheless provides a useful reminder that Canadian culture and social policy still often fail to reflect the contributions and needs of our polyethnic society.[32] But perhaps that merely means that the shape of this new society is still emerging and will never reach a final form. As Michael Ignatieff wrote recently in response to critics of multiculturalism: 'Our common cultural capital is not depleting: it is simply changing very rapidly, as our demographic composition, economic structure and technology change. Canada recurrently wakes up and doesn't recognize itself: there is nothing new about this'[33] Multiculturalism, as it develops in francophone and anglophone Canada, may ironically prove to be an unexpected bond in a new imagined community.

The most intractable of the issues I have discussed, I think, is the one relating to the First Nations. It is intractable because it is the most serious: relations between natives and newcomers began in conquest and dispossession leading to centuries of colonialism. The dimensions are cultural, economic, and political. That the relationship has begun to change, as exemplified in the Nisga'a settlement, Nunavut, and others, is certain. But what the new relationship will be ultimately – where the

First Nations will fit into a new imagined community – is far from predictable. The best that can be said is that there is no one model: the people involved are too varied in their social conditions, institutional development, and cultural autonomy. In *Citizens Plus*, Alan Cairns's lucid analysis of the evolution of constitutional policies and proposals relating to the place of native peoples in Canada, a powerful case is made for new arrangements that recognize the values both of Canadian citizenship and of distinctive Native cultures: 'pluralistic solidarity.' 'Both our separateness and our togetherness need to be institutionally supported,' Cairns concludes, 'if the overall Canadian community is to survive.'[34] Persuasive as this argument is, it is obvious that the river still has a very long way to run.

For all this, Canada in 2003 is potentially an imagined community of real communities that I would call postnationalist communities. Each community has its distinctive inheritance and outlook, but each is capable of membership in a wider community of shared civic values.[35] The Canadian Constitution of 1982, with its Charter of Rights and Freedoms, defines both the shared values of an ideal liberal democratic society and sets out the cultural and linguistic differences that should be entrenched, preserved, and promoted. It combines the universal and the particular that is the hallmark of postnationalism: neither Mill nor Herder but a recognition of the need for balance. *Métissages*, as the Quebec artist-performer Robert Lepage titled his recent multimedia, multicultural exhibition at Quebec's Musée de la Civilisation, is the word that best describes the character of postnationalist society. The same title could have been applied to a recent concert by the Toronto baroque orchestra Tafelmusik, which integrated traditional lutelike instruments from China (the *pipa*) and India (the *veena)* as well as Innuit throat singing by two members of Aqsarniit into an amazing performance of Vivaldi's *Four Seasons.* I think that *métissage* is what Yann Martel meant when he remarked, after winning the 2002 Booker Prize for his post-nationalist Canadian novel, *Life of Pi*, that 'Canada is, in many ways, the world ... the greatest hotel on earth.'[36]

The Canadian nation, then, is 'an imagined political community,' though not quite in Benedict Anderson's sense. The 'horizontal relationship' exists, but so do vertical relationships that nourish the different communities, some with a longer historical existence than others. A country both born and made, a nation of multiple identities.[37] Almost by definition such an imagined community of real communities remains unfinished and untidy, founded on the proposition expressed by the Irish philosopher Richard Kearney, in *Post Nationalist Ireland*, that 'cultural creation comes from hybridization not purity, contamination not immunity, polyphony not monologue.'[38]

NOTES

1 Anthony D. Smith, *Nationalism and Modernism* (London and New York: Routledge, 1998) and *Theories of Nationalism*, 2nd ed. (London: Duckworth, 1971).

2 Anthony D. Smith, 'Gastronomy or Geology? The Role of Nationalism in the Reconstruction of Nations,' *Nations and Nationalism* 1, no. 1 (1995): 3–24.

3 Liah Greenfield, *Nationalism: Five Roads to Modernity* (Cambridge: Harvard University Press, 1992).

4 John Stuart Mill, *A System of Logic* (London: Harper & Brothers, 1862), vi, 10; Ernest Renan, *Qu'est-ce qu'une nation?* (Paris: Imprimerie nationale, 1996), 47–9; Lord Acton, *Essays on Freedom and Power* (Gloucester, MA: P. Smith, 1972), 141–70.

5 Robert R. Ergang, *Herder and the Foundations of German Nationalism* (New York: Octagon Books, 1966), 150, 243–4. In his sympathetic, even apologetic, discussion of Herder in *Three Critics of the Enlightenment: Vico, Hamann, Herder* (Princeton, NJ: Princeton University Press, 2000), 169–242, Isaiah Berlin argues that Herder was a 'cultural,' not a 'political,' nationalist, though he admits that the German clergyman's writings contain many contradictions. Berlin also allows that Herder's thought may have 'been the first stage of a development destined in its later stages to become nationalistic and chauvinistic in the full, aggressive sense' (206), but insists that Herder cannot be held responsible for these later uses of his thought. That claim is unconvincing, as Joan Cocks argues in *Passion and Paradox* (Princeton, NJ: Princeton University Press, 2002), 108–10.

6 Anthony D. Smith, *The Ethnic Origins of Nations* (Oxford: Blackwell, 1986). Even the issue of 'ethnie,' on which Smith bases his claims for the pre-nation origin of nations, is open to question, as Patrick J. Geary's *The Myth of Nations* (Princeton, NJ: Princeton University Press, 2003) demonstrates.

7 E.J. Hobsbawm, *Nations and Nationalism since 1780* (New York: Cambridge University Press, 1990); Hobsbawn's account is disputed, with some effect, in Adrian Hastings, *The Construction of Nationhood: Ethnicity, Religion and Nationalism* (Cambridge: Cambridge University Press, 1997).

8 Elie Kedourie, *Nationalism* (London: Hutchinson, 1960).

9 Walker Connor, *Ethnonationalism: The Quest for Understanding* (Princeton, NJ: Princeton University Press, 1994), esp. chs. 4 and 8.

10 Eugen Weber, *Peasants into Frenchmen: The Modernization of Rural France, 1870–1914* (Stanford: Stanford University Press, 1976). For a brilliant study of the manner in which one nation – Israel – constructs itself and unintentionally provokes the emergence of a second nation – Palestine – see Meron Benvenisti, *Sacred Landscape: The Buried History of the Holy Land since 1948* (Berkeley: University of California Press, 2000), esp. ch. 6.

11 Maurizio Viroli, *For the Love of Country: An Essay on Patriotism and Nationalism* (Oxford: Clarendon Press, 1995), 1. See also Connor, *Ethnonationalism*, 196. For a critique of this position see Bernard Yack, 'The Myth of the Civic Nation,' and Nicholas Xenos, 'Civic Nationalism: Oxymoron,' in *Critical Review* 10, no. 2 (1966): 193–212 and 213–32.

12 Eugen Weber, 'The Future of Nationalism,' *Critical Review* 10, no. 2 (1996): 292. Evidence of nationalist 'aggression' is readily at hand. See, for example, Mark Mazower, *Dark Continent: Europe's Twentieth Century* (New York: Knopf, 2000), and Norman N. Naimark, *Fires of Hatred: Ethnic Cleansing in the Twentieth Century* (Cambridge: Harvard University Press, 2001).

13 *Benedict Anderson, Imagined Communities: Reflections on the Origins and Spread of Nationalism*, rev. ed. (London: Verso, 1991).

14 Ramsay Cook, *Provincial Autonomy, Minority Rights and the Compact Theory, 1867–1921* (Ottawa: Queen's Printer, 1969).

15 R.G. Haliburton, *The Men of the North and Their Place in History: A Lecture* (Montreal, 1869); Carl Berger, 'The True North Strong and Free,' in Peter Russell, ed., *Nationalism in Canada* (Toronto: McGraw-Hill, 1966), 3–26; John Ralston Saul, *Reflections of a Siamese Twin: Canada at the End of the Twentieth Century* (Toronto: Viking, 1997). Sherrill E. Grace's *Canada and the Idea of North* (Montreal: McGill-Queen's University Press 2002), the most thorough, though uncritical, study of this nationalist ideology, is yet another example of the continuing attraction of this idea. The confusions and ironies of the northern myth are brilliantly dissected in Janice Cavell, 'The Second Frontier: The North in English-Canadian Historical Writing,' *Canadian Historical Review* 83, no. 3 (2002): 364–89.

16 Carl Berger, *The Sense of Power* (Toronto: University of Toronto Press, 1970); Ramsay Cook, *Canada, Quebec and the Uses of Nationalism* (Toronto: McClelland and Stewart, 1995), 172–95.

17 Cook, *Canada, Quebec*, 85–97.

18 Ibid., 118–36.

19 Guy Laforest, *Trudeau et la fin d'un rêve canadien* (Sillery, QC: Septentrion, 1992).

20 Charles Taylor, *Multiculturalism* (Princeton, NJ: Princeton University Press, 1994); Will Kymlicka, *Multicultural Citizenship* (Oxford: Clarendon Press, 1995). In 'Francophonia Forever,' *Times Literary Supplement*, 23 July 1999, 12–15, Andy Lamy raises some important questions about Charles Taylor's multicultural formulation. A poll conducted for the Washington-based Pew Research Center in 44 countries found that only in Canada did a significant majority (77%) express a favourable view towards immigrants. *Globe and Mail*, 5 December 2002, A19.

21 Serge Cantin, 'Pour sortir de la survivance,' *Le Devoir*, 14 August 1999; Fernand Dumont, *Genèse de la société québecoise* (Montreal: Boréal 1993), 276–7. See also Mathieu Bock-Côté, 'Pour une pensée conservatrice: Contre l'ethique démocratique dans la compréhension de l'identité nationale québécoise,' *Horizons philosophiques* (Spring 2002): 57–73. In his response to the narrow defeat of the sovereignty option in the referendum of 30 October 1995 (50.58% No, 49.4% Yes), then premier Jacques Parizeau declared: 'C'est vrai qu'un a eté battu, mais au fond, pourquoi? Par l'argent et les votes éthniques. Des gens ont eu tellement peur que la tentation de se venger les mois qui viennent sera quelque chose.' *La Presse*, 31 October 1995. For a critical assessment of the PQ's sovereignty program see Jan Penrose, '"Mon pays ce n'est pas un pays": The Concept of Nation as a Nationalist Challenge to the Nationalist Aspirations of the Parti Québécois,' *Political Geography* 13, no. 2 (1995): 161–81, and 'Essential Constructions? The "Cultural Bases" of Nationalist Movements,' *Nations and Nationalism* 1, no. 3 (1995): 391–418.

22 Gérard Bouchard, 'Manifest pour une coalition nationale,' *Le Devoir*, 4 September 1999; *La nation québécoise au futur et au passé* (Montreal: VLB, 1999); *Dialogue sur les Pays* (Montreal: Boréal, 1999), 164. Jocelyn Létourneau's essay, 'Passer d'héritiers à fondateurs,' in *Passer á l'avenir* (Montreal: Boréal, 2000), 43–78, is a perceptive critique of Bouchard's project. For a literary expression of multiculturalism in Quebec see Monique Proulx, *Aurora Montrealis* (Toronto: Douglas and McIntyre, 1997).

23 Robert Comeau and Bernard Dionne, eds., *A propos de l'histoire nationale* (Quebec: Septentrion, 1998), especially the chapters by Lucia Ferretti and Gérard Bouchard.

24 J.L. Granatstein, *Who Killed Canadian History?* (Toronto: HarperCollins, 1998), 149.

25 *To the Source*, Commissioners' Report, First Nations Circle on the Constitution (Ottawa: Assembly of First Nations, 1992). See Alan C. Cairns, 'Aboriginal Canadians, Citizenship and the Constitution' (unpublished paper, 1994), 10–13.

26 Cook, ibid., cited 81.

27 *Sovereign Injustice* (Nemaska: Grand Council of the Crees of Quebec, 1995), n.p.

28 Lysianne Gagnon, 'Sovereignty Is Not Dead, Just Sleeping,' *Globe and Mail*, 11 November 2002, A15; André Pratte, 'Quebec's Quiet Counter-revolution, *Globe and Mail*, 7 November 2002, A 23; *Globe and Mail*, 22 November, 1999, A1 and A4; for polls, see *Globe and Mail*, 31 March 2000 A8: No 57.2%, Yes 42.8% (sovereignty with economic partnership) and *Globe and Mail*, 6 September 2002, A6: No 65%, Yes 35%. Maurice Pinard, Robert Bernier, Vincent Lemieux, *Un Combat inachevé* (Sainte-Foy: Presses de l'Université du Québec, 1997), and Maurice Pinard, 'The Political Universe of Ambivalent Francophone Voters,' *Opinion Canada* 6, no. 4 (1998). For contrasting opinions on the prospects for Quebec see *Policy Options*, 21, no. 5 (2000): 8–45. This ambiguity, I once argued, is the most persistent characteristic of nationalism in Quebec. See 'The Paradox of Quebec,' in Cook, ibid., 98–109.

29 *Globe and Mail*, 27 December 1999, reporting Jack Jedwab's *Ethnic Identification and Heritage Languages in Canada.*

30 Reed Scowan, *Time to Say Goodbye: The Case for Getting Quebec out of Canada* (Toronto: McClelland and Stewart, 1999).

31 Jocelyn Létourneau, 'Assumons l'identité québécoise dans sa complexité,' *Le Devoir*, 7 August 1999.

32 Veronica Strong-Boag et al., eds., *Painting the Maple: Essays on Race, Gender and the Construction of Canada* (Vancouver: UBC Press, 2000).

33 See a report based on 2001 census data on the composition of Canada's population see *Globe and Mail*, 22 January 2003, A6; Michael Ignatieff, 'Historians Exaggerate the Importance of History,' *National Post*, 4 September 2000; Will Kymlicka, *Finding Our Way: Rethinking Ethnocultural Relations in Canada*, (Toronto: Oxford University Press, 1998), 15–123. In *The Illusion of Difference* (Toronto: C.D. Howe Institute, 1994) Jeffrey Reitz and Raymond Breton argue that ethnic differences between multicultural Canada and the U.S. 'melting pot' are greatly exaggerated. See also Pico Iyer, *The Global Soul* (New York 2000), 115–72, for an outsider's positive assessment of multicultural Toronto; for negative assessments from contrasting viewpoints see Daniel Stoffman, *Who Gets In* (Toronto: Macfarlane Walter & Ross, 2002), 119–150, and Himani Bannerji, *The Dark Side of the Nation* (Toronto: Canadian Scholars' Press, 2000), 87–124.

34 Alan C. Cairns, *Citizens Plus: Aboriginal Peoples and the Canadian State* (Vancouver: UBC Press, 2000), 212.

35 For a more theoretical discussion of these contentions see Jürgen Habermas, 'The European Nation-State: On the Past and Future of Sovereignty

and Citizenship,' in *The Inclusion of the Other*, ed. Ciaran Cronin and Pablo De Grieff (Cambridge, Mass.: MIT Press, 1999), 105–27.

36 Introducing his exhibition, Lepage wrote 'cette thématique allait m'entraîner bien au-delà des considerations culturelles et me faire comprendre que la réalité du métissage implique jusqu'à la moindrefibre de ce qui constitue notre identité. Tous ces voyages, tous ces projets lointains ... qui devaient m'éloigner de mes origines n'ont finalement eu pour effet que de me ramener chez moi, transformé, mais authentique.' *Métissages*, Salle de presse Archives, Musée de la civilisation à Québec. See also Kate Taylor, 'Crossing borders and breeds in Quebec,' *Globe and Mail*. 23 May 2000; B5. *Tafelmusik* 27 November to 1 December 2002 program, 'The Four Seasons: A Cycle of the Sun.' Yann Martel's remark was broadcast on CBC radio, 24 October, 2002.

37 Ramsay Cook, 'Identities Are Not Like Hats,' *Canadian Historical Review* 81, 2 (2000): 260–6.

38 Richard Kearney, *Post Nationalist Ireland* (London and New York: Routledge, 1997), 101. Patrick Geary concludes in his *The Myth of Nations*, ibid., 156–7, that the history of Europe 'is not the story of a primordial moment but of a continuous process' and that today, as in the past, 'the peoples of Europe are a work in progress and always must be.'

Closing the Nation: Nationalism and Statism in Nineteenth- and Twentieth-Century Germany

DIETMAR SCHIRMER

In academic as well as in public discourse, it is widely agreed that the German brand of nationalism is determined by the idea of ethno-cultural homogeneity. This *völkisch* tradition emerged from the romantic roots of German nationalism in the late eighteenth and early nineteenth centuries, *prior* to the existence of a German state.[1] It is exemplified by the citizenship law of 1913, which made *jus sanguinis* – the principle of common descent – the sole and determining principle of membership in the state.[2] The law of 1913, and thus the ethno-cultural character of Germanness, remained by and large intact until very recently. It is also generally agreed that in postwar West Germany, the law of 1913 not only served as a tool for extending the citizenship of the Federal Republic to the citizens of the German Democratic Republic (GDR) and to people of German descent living in the countries of Central and Eastern Europe, but also organized the exclusionary treatment of several generations of labour immigrants. Now, in the years following German unification, a surge of xenophobic activities primarily in, but not limited to, East Germany has brought ethno-cultural nationalism and racism under renewed scrutiny, both in Germany and abroad.

The broad contours of this master narrative of German nationalism are beyond dispute. However, the argument put forward in this paper will be that the preceding narrative presents an incomplete interpretation of the history of German 'nation-ness,' with the result that contemporary discourses on this issue fail to account for analytically as well as prescriptively important aspects of the story. I will argue that in order to thoroughly understand matters of inclusion and exclusion in Germany, we must attend to another source of political integration. This source is what we might call statism.[3] The statist rationale grants or withholds membership rights not on the grounds of ethno-cultural homogeneity (as ethnic nationalism does), and not on the grounds of place of birth or extended residence (as civic nationalism does), but rather on the principles of presumed loyalty or disloyalty to the state.

My case in point is the debate surrounding the citizenship reform legislation proposed in 1999 by the coalition government of Social Democrats and Greens. Citizenship reform was a signature policy of the new government; both parties had stated clearly their reform policies in their individual election platforms as well as in the coalition treaty that outlined their legislative agenda. The citizenship reform proposal consisted of two main parts, one concerning changes of citizenship, the other concerning naturalization laws. With respect to citizenship, the children of long-term residents of foreign nationality were to be given German citizenship by right of birth. In other words, the governing majority proposed to inject a solid dose of *jus soli*, territorial law, into the traditionally *jus sanguinis*-based concept of German citizenship. With respect to naturalization, the project aimed to lower the barriers, first by adjusting the standards, and second – and more importantly – by generally accepting dual citizenship instead of making naturalization contingent on the applicant surrendering his or her original citizenship.[4]

But in the spring of 1999 the Red-Green government lost the state elections in Hesse and, consequently, its majority in the *Bundesrat*, the upper house of Parliament. This defeat was preceded by an unusually nasty electoral campaign on the part of the opposition Christian Democratic Union (CDU), which focused on denouncing the citizenship reform program and made little effort to conceal its appeal to the electorate's xenophobic impulses. Thus, in order to get anything passed in the legislature, the government had to negotiate a compromise with the parties of the centre-right.

All of this ensued at a time when there was broad consensus, challenged only by the nationalist fringes of the conservative parties, that some sort of citizenship reform was long overdue. In 1996, 7.3 million foreign nationals accounted for 8.9 per cent of the German resident population. Of these – even by the most conservative account – roughly 5 million people had to be considered permanent residents. Yet, throughout the first half of the 1990s, the number of naturalizations hovered around a meager 30,000.[5] Thus, a considerable part of the population remained deprived of political citizenship rights – a fact that obviously posed a problem of democratic legitimacy and political representation.

The compromise legislation, which was signed into law in the summer of 1999, differed from the original proposal in one key respect: it did not allow dual citizenship. Instead, it made a person's naturalization contingent on the rejection of her or his original citizenship. It also obliged third-generation children of immigrants, who henceforth would acquire German citizenship by birth, to decide between the ages of eighteen and twenty-three which citizenship – German, or that of their parents – they would maintain permanently.[6]

If one were to assume that ethno-culturalism offers a sufficient explanation for the German concept of nation-ness, one might have expected the major line of conflict in the debate on the Red-Green reform package to occur where a truly new feature was being proposed. This new feature was the element of *jus soli*, which gives third-generation immigrants access to German citizenship by right of birth. Instead, the conflict escalated over the issue of dual citizenship, focusing on questions pertaining to military service, diplomatic representation, and other issues relating to membership in the state rather than the ethnic nation. Thus, the opponents of a fundamental reform of citizenship have apparently been less concerned with the preservation of any fictional ethno-cultural purity of the *Volk* than with perceptions of loyalty or disloyalty to the state.

This essay's argument will proceed in four main steps. It will start with an account of how, beginning in the late eighteenth and early nineteenth centuries, the German nation was constructed as the organic entity of the *Volk*. Based on the romantic idea of organic solidarity and linguistic community, this construction was in opposition to the supposedly mechanistic solidarity of the contractual notion of civic nations.[7] Second, we will trace the evolution and the characteristics of Prussian and German statism. We will find that for much of the nineteenth century, the two notions of ethno-nationalism and statism were not congruent, contrary to the Gellnerian definition of the national principle as the demand for congruence between state and nation.[8] Third, we will examine how and to what effect the *Reich* of 1871, for the first time in modern German history, forced the principles of nationalism and statism into congruency. The evidence suggests that the merging of those two principles resulted in a dramatic closing of the lens on matters of membership rights.

Fourth, we will touch briefly on the relationship between nationalism and statism in the Weimar Republic and the Nazi state, before we return to the contemporary discourse on nationhood and citizenship.

The chapter will probe the extent to which this discourse is still organized by tensions between the statist and ethno-nationalist rationales of inclusion and exclusion.

I

The intellectual movement of early German nationalism was the illegitimate child of two experiences that deeply affected the legitimacy of the absolutist political orders of the German states. Both these experiences had a French dimension. One was the triumph of the European Enlightenment and its scientific, analytical world view, which undermined the validity of religion and mythology and, consequently, the doctrine of divine right. The other was the French Revolution, which in its imperial phase culminated in the temporary hegemony of Napoleon and his armies over most of Europe – a hegemony that included the annexation or occupation of the many Germanies of the time. The experience of foreign occupation between 1804 and 1815 determined that German nationalism had, from its onset, the negative character of an anti–foreign liberation nationalism.

The intellectual impact of the French Revolution on Germany and its intellectuals was immediate but highly ambiguous. Bernhard Giesen characterizes the response of the German educated classes to the French Revolution as a sequence of 'enthusiasm and disappointment,'[9] parallelling the revolution's turn from its constitutional-monarchic phase to that of the Jacobin terror. Initially, it seemed that in revolutionary France

> the patriotic idea of a society without corporate inequalities, geared entirely towards virtue and rationality, was realized to a much greater degree than in the enlightened Prussia of Frederick II. The enthusiasm of the German educated classes for the revolutionary project in France is well known: It was common to travel to Paris and found Jacobin clubs; the repercussions of the Revolution in the work of many great intellectuals are obvious.[10]

Even from the distance of more than a quarter-century, old Hegel, in the concluding chapter of his *Vorlesungen über die Philosophie der Geschichte*, emphatically celebrated the French Revolution as 'a glorious sunrise':

> Never since the sun had stood in the firmament and the planets revolved around him has it been perceived that man turns himself onto his head, i.e.

on Thought, and molds reality according to Thought ... This was accordingly a glorious sunrise. All thinking beings shared in the jubilation of this epoch. Emotions of a lofty character stirred men's minds at that time; a spiritual enthusiasm thrilled through the world, as if the reconciliation between the Divine and the Secular was now first accomplished.[11]

Yet even the initial enthusiasm over the dawn of freedom in neighbouring France did not create any sense of urgency, or even legitimacy, for a revolutionary project in Germany. In France, the revolution had swept away an *ancien régime* that was unwilling and unable to reform; in contrast, in the eyes of contemporaries, reform absolutism in the Germanies had already proven its capacity for reform and self-renewal. Were not the rational bureaucracies of the small German states superior to the inefficient, arbitrary, and wasteful French central administration? Was not the slow and steady process of top-down reform highly preferable to the inherently risky course of a bottom-up revolution with entirely uncertain results? Thus, the French case, even in its initial phase, was rarely taken as an appropriate model for Germany. Instead, Germany was to proceed 'without nonsense, without anarchy ... with gentle reforms.'[12] Why? Because 'Germany is more than any other European state in the mood for revolutions of the spirit, and least for political revolutions.'[13] This general restraint, mixed with a sense of German superiority vis-à-vis the anachronism of the French *ancien régime*, and in combination with a constraining socio-political framework, kept the train of political development firmly on the tracks of reform absolutism.[14]

Thus, on the one hand, despite the initial enthusiasm of the educated classes, the French Revolution could not trigger anything resembling a revolutionary situation in Germany. On the other hand, the dark sides of the French Revolution – the Jacobin terror and Bonapartism – demonstrated that Enlightenment rationality had not only done away with older forms of feudal despotism, but also eroded the very foundations of a transcendental legitimization of state, society, and individual existence. The early romantic movement of the late eighteenth century, as represented by the names and works of Herder, Lessing, Schlegel, Schiller, and Novalis, responded to this existential alienation with a critique of analytic rationality and with demands for the creation of a 'new religion' or a 'new mythology' as a counter-program to the 'mechanical' age that was dawning in France.[15] An anonymous, untitled treatise, probably written in 1796,[16] put it the following way: 'Only that which is the subject of freedom, we call idea. We therefore have to move beyond the state! – Because each state has to treat free human beings as mechanical gear; and this he shall not, he shall therefore cease to be.' And it continues after a few paragraphs: 'Primarily, I want to speak of an idea, which, as far as I know, has not come to anybody's mind – we have to have a new mythology, yet this mythology must be to the service of the ideas, it must become a mythology of reason.'[17] The impulse of this new mythology was not so much antimodern or antirational – 'a mythology of reason' – but rather one that involved surpassing analytical rationality by reintegrating it in and submitting it to a higher, synthetic idea.[18]

From the dichotomy analysis versus synthesis we derive a whole syntactic series of other dichotomies, ones which were to occupy German romantic and nationalist discourse for the next two centuries: mechanism versus organicism, society versus community, modernity versus the medieval. Most importantly, in Schlegel's and Humboldt's philosophy of language, the dichotomy of synthesis and analysis was applied to a normative typology of languages. This typology attributed supreme value to the more synthetic and inflected languages, such as Latin and German, while regarding the more analytic languages, such as French and English, as decadent forms. This is significant for two reasons. First and obviously, in the absence of a unified German state, language was already the constitutive criterion of nation-ness and Volksgeist – 'Thus every nation speaks as it thinks and thinks as it speaks,' as Herder had put it,[19] and, likewise, Uhland: 'He, who does not respect and love his language, can neither respect nor love his people; he, who does not understand his language, can neither understand his people and can never feel what the real German virtue and glory is; because in the depth of language is hidden all inner understanding and all authentic character of the people.'[20] Second, the distinction between synthetic and analytic languages provides the crucial link between the Romantic idea of ethno-cultural nationhood and the creation of a hierarchical order of nations. This pattern was later exploited to rank nations and races – with, of course, the Germans coming out on top.

Herder's Ideas on the Philosophy of the History of Humanity (1784–91) presented a philosophy of history – at the time, a popular subject – that depicted history as a natural process. Here we can glean a radical inversion of Kantian Enlightenment philosophy: nature, not reason, makes the world go round. And presumably, it is within nature and natural conditions that cultures evolve and are shaped. As a consequence, Herder organizes those chapters which deal with mankind's 'different appearances' according to regions defined by geography and climate – that is, a rough taxonomic system of the natural conditions of cultural evolution.[21]

Herder's concept of rooting or embedding human existence in the supposedly authentic ways of tradition, culture, and soil set the tone for the further development of ethno-cultural nationalism. This tone sharpened and hardened in the wake of the French occupation and the Wars of Liberation, during which we see the emergence of a small nationalist movement. Nationalism was still largely confined to intellectual circles, but now it featured an entirely different crowd of spokespeople, including Ernst Moritz Arndt, Theodor Körner, and the *Turnvater* Friedrich Ludwig Jahn, the founder of the German gymnastics movement. At this point the German Romantic movement evolved into rabid German nationalism and anti-French agitation. All of this happened more or less within the Romantic mode of thought. Herder's fairly benign ethno-culturalism was now transformed into a rigid hierarchy of nations and races: an ethno-cultural nationalism that was both dismissive of and aggressive toward everything foreign, and that was unifying in a heroic-existential and, eventually, militaristic manner with respect to its area of inclusion.

After the occupation of German lands by Napoleon's armies, the nation and the fatherland seemed on the verge of decline and even dissolution. Against this elemental threat, and consistent with the Romantic rooting of the *Volk* in its mythological past, nationalist agitators of the early nineteenth century set out to mobilize their contemporaries by reminding them of the heroism of their ancient and medieval ancestors. Thus, the struggles of the Germanic tribes (against Roman occupation), of the medieval Holy Roman Empire of the German nation, and of the Protestant Reformation (against Rome) – personified respectively by Herman, Barbarossa, and Martin Luther – were established as founding myths of the nation and as moral and patriotic examples for contemporaries. Johann Gottlieb Fichte, holder of the most prominent German chair in philosophy in Berlin, concluded his 'Addresses to the German Nation' of 1808 with the following call to patriotic duty:

Think that in my voice there are mingled the voices of your ancestors of the hoary past, who with their own bodies stemmed the onrush of Roman world dominion, who with their blood won the independence of those mountains, plains, and rivers, which under you have fallen prey to the foreigner ... Then, too, there mingle with these voices the spirits of your more recent forefathers, those who fell in the holy war for freedom of belief and religion. 'Save our honor too,' they cry to you ... It is for you to justify and give meaning to our sacrifice, by setting this spirit to fulfill its purpose and to rule the world' ... There comes a solemn appeal to you from your descendants yet unborn. 'You boast of your forefathers,' they cry to you, 'and link yourselves with pride to a noble line. Take care that the chain does not break off with you; see to it that we, too, may boast of you and use you as an unsullied link to connect ourselves with the same illustrious line. Do not force us to be ashamed of our descent from you as from base and slavish barbarians; do not force us to conceal our origin, or to fabricate a strange one and to take a strange name, lest we be at once and without further examination rejected and trodden underfoot.'[22]

In this way, the transformation of assorted historical myths and diverse historical episodes into a coherent and consistent national narrative, one that exalted past heroes and called for future ones, became one of the two main pillars of German national consciousness. The second, of course, was language. Take, for instance, Arndt's popular song 'What Is the German's Fatherland?' a fixture of the *Nationalfeste* that became pervasive all over Germany between 1813 and 1848. In the first six of its seven verses, the singer of the German nation lays out the different German lands, each time followed by the exclamation, 'Oh no, no, no, [the German's] fatherland must be larger.' The last verse goes:

> What is the German's fatherland?
> So, finally, tell me which land it shall be!
> As far as the German tongue is spoken,
> And God in heaven sings his songs,
> This shall it be! This, brave German, call your own:
> The whole of Germany shall it be!'[23]

These were the basic materials that the Romantic movement used to construct the German nation: a historical narrative presented as a national genealogy; and language as the chord binding the German *Volk* together and marking the territory of the German nation. If we had space to explore this in greater depth, we could demonstrate that the method of distinguising between one's own nation and the foreign was basically the same one that the earlier Romantic movement had applied in order to distinguish between Romanticism and Enlightenment thought – synthesis versus analysis, organicism versus mechanism, community versus society – but now syntactically expanded to include dichotomies such as East and West, German and French, culture and civilization, authentic and decadent, and so on. Thus, we see that the original distinction, which had referred to different intellectual movements, was being culturalized, territorialized, nationalized, and employed hierarchically and thus transformed into a new, nationalist distinction between the German and the foreign. The syntactic system of Romanticism versus Enlightenment thinking and German versus non-German contained the whole universe of the national self-stereotyping of the Germans vis-à-vis their French, and later also their English and Russian neighbours, and thus stimulated the creation of an elaborate system of national stereotypes.[24]

II

Germany? But where is it? I do not know where to find this country.
Where the learned Germany begins, the political Germany ends.
Goethe/Schiller, Xenien, 1796

The ethno-cultural trajectory of early nineteenth-century German nationalism should not surprise us, given that no German state was at hand that could have contained both the nation and national sentiment. Thus, part of the explanation for ethno-cultural and civic nationalism revolves around a structure of opportunity and constraint: civic concepts of nationhood seem to correlate with a historical sequence that goes from state to nation; ethno-cultural nations seem to prevail where the sequence is reversed.[25] However, I would argue that the German version of nationalism has a second important source, which I will call statism.[26] Its historical roots are Prussian rather than German. The period of its emergence as an institution is bracketed by the Prussian General Code of 1794 and the constitutionalization of Prussia in the course of the arrested revolution of 1848, and thus includes the Prussian reform era of 1807 to 1819.

German nationalism and the reformed version of Prussian statism evolved roughly around the same time, yet they did so incongruously; this is why Goethe found that the 'learned' – read *cultural* – Germany begins where the 'political' – read *statist* – ends. Of course, the national movement of the early nineteenth century did not occur in a stateless space; rather, the German states, and Prussia in particular, were in certain respects well developed and generally not lacking in modernity compared to their European neighbours. Consequently, just as nationalism had to integrate the German nation without referring to a particular state, the existing states had to integrate their respective populations without the assistance of the concept of the German nation.

Prussia, in particular, was both culturally and territorially a highly contingent product of centuries of warfare, inheritance, *Machtpolitik*, and more warfare. Lacking any 'natural' geographic boundary, and lacking any kind of linguistic, historic, or religious homogeneity, it attempted to integrate its subjects around the central idea of the state. German idealism had laid the cornerstone of this project by conceptualizing the state with a capital S – the state as an end in itself rather than as a means to a particular social or political end, be it the common good or the good of the privileged classes or an individual ruler. What this means may become clearer if we contrast the 'L'etat c'est moi' of French absolutism with Frederick II's self-stylization as the 'state's first servant.' In the latter case, the state appears as an abstract idea – as *objektiver Geist* in Hegel's terms – that is not identical to and cannot be fully incorporated by any individual, or any social estate or class: 'Since the state is mind objectified, it is only as one of its members that the individual himself has objectivity, genuine individuality, and an ethical life.'[27] Within the logic of the corporate state, this rationale can easily be transformed into an affirmation of the hierarchical *status quo* and the abolition of freedom for the sake of the state: 'The supreme way man can put his freedom to use, and the only means to strengthen and expand it, is to subordinate himself, to be obedient, to serve, to become a part of the larger, the state. God is the creator of the states; He has decreed the division of the states and estates, as well as the uniting of the same states and estates.'[28]

When the state is cast as an abstract idea and a transcendental order, political integration becomes, as Gregg Kvistad argues, a function of the relative proximity of individuals or social classes to that unattainable centre which is the spirit of the state.[29] Estates or classes turn around this imaginary centre like planets around the sun, some of them closer and some of them farther away. The more of the unattainable spirit – *Geist* – of the state a concrete individual carries in the attainable form of conviction – *Gesinnung* – the closer that individual approaches the centre. In democratic nation-states, membership is spelled out as citizenship, whereby all members are defined as equals relative to the state; in contrast, here we find a model of concentric integration that distinguishes between degrees of membership, structured according to presumed loyalty to the state. The king as the 'state's first servant' has definitionally the highest loyalty status, followed by the officer corps, the civil servants, and the professional officials of the state. The fact that even the king himself and the definitionally loyal state servants can never embody the spirit of the state proper, but can only display a degree of loyalty that at best would be considered adequate, establishes the rationale for the permanent monitoring of state servants' convictions. This realm of definitional loyalty is, as the realm of the state, demarcated from the realm of society (i.e., the general population).[30]

The General Code's principled distinction between, on the one hand, the non-self-interested, non-propertied, and educated civil servants that populated the state realm and, on the other hand, the particularistic, self-interested activities of the societal sphere, was engendered and elaborated on during the era of Prussian reform. Thus, German liberalism took on, as Rudolf Vierhaus puts it, a 'governmental character.'[31] Everywhere else, liberalism was a political movement for limiting state power and guaranteeing the civil rights and liberties of individual citizens vis-à-vis the state. The mainstream of German liberalism rejected not only the sovereignty of the absolutist monarch, but also popular sovereignty as a 'particularistic' principle. Only 'state sovereignty' was considered free of self-interest and particularism. Consequently, German liberals embarked on the political ideology of the *Rechtsstaat*, the state of constitutional law, as the only form of state that could properly handle the highest good of all: sovereignty.

Compared to the state, the societal realm was conceptualized not only as a somewhat lower realm of particularistic interests, but also as a potentially anarchic realm that needed the guarding and ordering, healing and punishing hand of the state in order to form particularistic subjects into able and obedient state citizens. Only the revolutionary/counter-revolutionary cycle of 1848–9 and the deficient Prussian constitution imposed by Frederick William IV finally established a narrow slice of guaranteed political rights and civil liberties. This resulted in a gradual shift toward the definition of citizenship as an individual status vis-à-vis the state. However, it did not break the circle of statist logic, because it was accompanied by a sharp distinction between a higher realm of definitionally legitimate political activity carried out by definitionally loyal state servants and a lower, potentially illegitimate domain of political activity in civil society and the political parties. In July 1848, just after the revolutionary cycle of 1848–9 had begun to take its course, the Prussian conservative Ludwig von Gerlach clearly delineated the patriarchal character of the Prussian idea of the state, and contrasted it to what he considered to be the pagan, pantheistic, and perverted ideas of the nationalist movement:

> One does not consider that, as the father precedes the family as its source and root, do authority and the state precede the nation as its source and root. There has never been a nation that did not emerge from an authority, be it that of a ruler, a tribal leader or a lord of the manor. – It is, therefore, absurd, impossible, and contrary to the nature and the concept of nationality itself to dissolve the states into nationalities and declare the nationalities to be the foundations of new states.[32]

Even in the mid-1800s, the idea of statism would not have an iota of the nationalist principle. It insisted on the priority of the state, historically as well as ethically, and it considered state-making nationalism an absurdity. The statist idea left no room for the historical trajectory of 'nation to state.'

III

The statist principle was firmly in place by early in the nineteenth century. German nationalism moved – to apply Miroslav Hroch's stage model[33] – from the initial phase of nationalist agitation to its mass movement phase in the 1830s and 1840s.[34] We can assume that by around mid-century, at least the somewhat educated classes had been exposed to nationalist agitation to a substantial degree and had adopted some sort of national identity.[35] Around this time the Grimm Brothers were beginning to publish their famous German Dictionary, which like Martin Luther's Bible translation was an important milestone in the standardization and consolidation of written German. In the preface to the first volume of this dictionary, which was indeed intended to be a national monument, Jakob Grimm wrote: 'Beloved German countrymen, regardless what state, regardless what faith you may be, enter the great hall of your native, ancient language, which is open to all of you. Learn it and sanctify it and hold fast to it; your strength and endurance as a people rests in it.'[36]

'Regardless what state, regardless what faith ...' – by the mid-nineteenth century, with the devastating threat of foreign occupation gone, the ethno-cultural version of German nationalism had become quite inclusive: learn the language, make it your own, and be a part of the nation. In a sense, it was an invitation no less inclusive than the radically political mode of integration that was characteristic of the early phase of the French Revolution. Thus, at this point in time the two modes of membership – the rational membership in the state and the cultural membership in the nation – were each in their own way very inclusive. As we will see, this changed radically after 1871, once these two modes of membership were forced into congruency.

As a nation-state, the *Reich* founded after the Franco-Prussian War was a profoundly incomplete one. On the one hand, the Bismarck-*Reich*, the *kleindeutsche* – 'small German' – solution to the national question, was *not* the fatherland that Arndt and the other Romantic nationalists had imagined – 'as far as the German tongue is spoken.' On the other hand, the *Reich* was a federation of dynastic rulers under Prussian leadership, a functional association for economic advancement and the strengthening of international power, *not* a unitary nation-state, and certainly not the state of a sovereign people. The *Reich*'s constitution was emphatically federal, and *landsmannschaftliche* identities rooted in the smaller political units of the *Reich* remained strong – indeed, so strong that the army remained structured according to the member states. Moreover, until 1913 the *Reich* itself did not even have its own citizenship law. So, it is not surprising that its constitution did not once refer to the nation explicitly. In essence, the newly founded *Reich* oscillated between Prussian statist and German national ideas, unable to resolve the inherent tensions between them. As such, the *Reich* tended to corrupt the statist tradition of Prussian reform absolutism as well as the liberal tradition of nineteenth-century nationalism. Caught in the conflicting traditions of the universal *Reich* and the particularistic nation-state, it brought forth the worst of both worlds.[37]

Bismarck himself is more appropriately labelled a statist rather than a nationalist. He only turned toward nationalism opportunistically in pursuit of his Caesarist rule in an era of increasingly middle-class and, consequently, nationalist politics. He would become a part of the German national mythology only in retrospect, after his dismissal in 1890. That the Bismarck *Reich* treated matters of inclusion and exclusion largely according to the statist rationale of loyalty and disloyalty is evidenced by the two big exclusions of the era, the anti-Catholic *Kulturkampf* ('cultural struggle') of the 1870s and 1880s and the *Sozialistengesetze* (antisocialist laws) of 1878.

However, beginning in the late 1880s, the *Reich* – and the Prussian authorities in particular – also turned increasingly toward restrictive policies on matters of immigration and naturalization. The targets were primarily Polish workers, especially Polish Jews, many of whom had been living in Prussia for decades. For these people, the bureaucratic obstacles to naturalization became almost insurmountable.[38] Thus it can be argued that toward the end of Bismarck's tenure and after his dismissal, the two traditions of statism and ethno-cultural nationalism were finally brought into congruency; this had the effect of reshaping the politics of membership in a manner that was considerably more rigid and narrow than either the tradition of romantic nationalism or that of Prusso-German statism would have prescribed.

Clearly, the closing of the German nation, which was to find its legal form in the citizenship law of 1913, had its roots in the late 1880s and the 1890s. Indeed, in 1895 the *Reichstag* had already demanded that the government provide legislation concerning *Reich* citizenship. The ethno-cultural closing that the government and the conservative majority in the Imperial Diet championed should not, however, be interpreted exclusively in terms of a victory of Romantic nationalism over the statist tradition. Rather, it represents a combination of the *völkisch* principle of common blood and the statist principle of loyalty, but transformed to fit the needs of the imperialist policies that the Wilhelmine *Reich* had begun to pursue. Before 1913, citizenship had contained an odd combination of *jus sanguinis* and *jus soli* elements. One became a citizen by virtue of descent, and residence had little bearing on this. However, one could lose citizenship on the grounds of prolonged territorial absence. To make sense of this oddity, Gregg Kvistad suggests that it was the result of a combination of ethno-culturalism and statism, as a prolonged absence of ten years or more was considered proof of disloyalty. However, by the 1890s, when 'the German Reich ... had acquired many formal and even more numerous informal imperialist outposts, where Germans or non-Germans of German descent played an important role as agents of German economic and political interests,'[39] the practice of punishing prolonged absence from the *Reich* with the revocation of citizenship rights became dysfunctional.

Consequently, the citizenship law of 1913 not only eliminated the threat of revoking citizenship rights on grounds of sustained absence, but even made German-ness transmittable from generation to generation, without the *Reichsbürger* even having to set foot on the *Reich*'s territory. Thus, the *jus sanguinis* of the law of 1913 might best be interpreted as an adaptation of the ethno-culturalist *and* the statist traditions to a new set of historical conditions.

All of this decoupled German-ness from the German nation-state. Of course, if German-ness is deterritorialized, so that those in possession of it cannot lose it regardless of their conditions, the reverse must also be true: whoever does not have German blood cannot acquire German-ness, no matter how hard he or she tries. Prussia had proven the point, the argument went, when it failed to assimilate the Poles residing in its eastern territories: Why should one assume that immigrant Poles would fare better?

By fusing *völkisch*-Romantic with imperialist-statist principles, the law of 1913 marked the decisive disjuncture in the history of German nationhood. We therefore can afford to touch only briefly on the Weimar Republic and the Nazi *Reich*. It may be useful, however, to make a few points that illustrate the extent to which the statist principle carried over from the Wilhelmine era into the Weimar Republic and even into the Nazi state.

First, Wilhelmine civil servants have received quite some credit from historians for accepting, however grudgingly, the Republican outcomes of the November Revolution of 1918 and for taking a predominantly loyal stance toward the new Republican government. Of course, this loyalty was loyalty to the abstract state, not the concrete Republican order. The Baron von Stein, a self-described 'old Monarchist' and a higher civil servant before as well as after the war, later recounted: 'Having to work alongside people who until recently had been on the other side of the trench had a bitter and sour taste.' However, he overcame this, knowing 'that there is something higher, above the constitutional form of the state: the State himself.'[40] Thus, the civil servants were by no means turning into Republicans. Their statist identity, however, allowed them to operate above petty party quarrelling, which – in their minds and in the minds of many Germans – was all that the new order amounted to.

Second, the same statist loyalty worked to the advantage of the Third Reich after Hitler rose to power in January 1933. Systematic cleansing of the bureaucratic-administrative complex was largely restricted to the comparatively small number of Republican civil servants that had been appointed during the Weimar period and to the ranks of the political civil servants, who were either dismissed or forced into early retirement. Among the regular civil servants, the cleansing affected only an estimated 10 per cent of the highest and very few of the lower ranks.[41]

Third, it should be noted that the first major piece of anti-Semitic legislation came in the guise of the 'Law on the Restitution of the Professional Civil Service' of April 1933. The law was double-edged in a way that, once more, highlights the exclusionary effects of the combination of statist and ethnic/racist principles. As one especially infamous commentator, the presiding judge of the *Volksgerichtshof* (people's court), Freisler, put it: '*Racially and ideologically* alien elements were eliminated from the civil service.'[42]

This law was aimed at Jews, although at the insistence of President Hindenburg an exception was made for Jewish war veterans. At the same time, it was aimed at the so-called 'party-book *Beamte*,' the Republican civil servants who had been appointed during the Republican decade. The law fused the racist rationale of German national purity with the statist rationale of the civil service as occupying a realm above self-interest and political particularism. The fact that in this early phase of the Nazi system Hindenburg could still push through the exception for Jews who had proven their loyalty in war only reinforces this interpretation.

Finally, the characteristic conjunction of the two conditions of membership – blood and allegiance – also appears in the *Reich* Citizenship Law of 1935: 'Para. 2, sec. 1. Only the state citizen of German or of kindred blood who by his conduct proves that he is willing and able loyally to serve the German people and the Reich is a Reich citizen.'[43] The fusion of these two principles – state membership defined in terms of assumed loyalty or disloyalty, and membership in the German nation defined in terms of race and ethnicity – had been in the making for a century. Here it was completed.

IV

After the Second World War and with the emergence of the Cold War and the formation of two ideologically antagonistic German states, nation and state in Germany returned to their historically normal relationship – that is, incongruity. The Federal Republic, pushed by anti-Communist and Bolshevist *angst*, and pulled by the material rewards of capitalism and by Adenauer's and the Western Allies' policy of integration with the West, became, finally, an almost unambiguously Western European state. However, the westernization of West Germany should not be confused with the disappearance of the two traditional modes of integration – that of the statist differentiation between loyalty and disloyalty, and that of the ethno-cultural distinction between insiders and outsiders.

In the Federal Republic, the statist principle continued to organize the relations between state and civil service as a vertical differentiation between definitionally loyal civil servants and the potentially disloyal realm of civil society. Against the expressed will of the Allies, the government and Parliament of the emerging West German state succeeded in almost completely restoring the *Beamtentum* in its traditional sense.[44]

Like the statist rationale, the ethno-cultural version of *nation-ness* and citizenship based on *jus sanguinis* were swiftly restored in postwar West Germany, with a twofold result. First, after the racist and imperialist excesses of the Nazi period, ethno-culturalism and membership by descent turned into principles of territorial concentration rather than enlargement. In contrast to the Wilhelmine Empire, the Federal Republic during the Cold War used *jus sanguinis* not as a tool for extending its citizenship *beyond* its territorial boundaries to its cultural and imperial outposts, but rather to accommodate *within* the territory of the West German state those ethnic Germans who had been displaced by war and by the subsequent territorial realignments. Second, as in the *Reich* of 1871, ethno-culturalism and *jus sanguinis* in Germany became shields for protecting ethnic purity, by controlling and restricting immigration and by denying foreign residents access to full citizenship status. While it is true that naturalization procedures became less daunting over time,[45] the ethno-culturalism of *jus sanguinis* was to remain firmly in place until the citizenship reform of 1999.

The more recent German debates on nation-ness and national identity present the following main alternatives: on the one hand, there has been the reanimation of the Bismarckian combination of ethno-culturalist nationalism and statist *Machtpolitik* in the wake of unification; on the other hand, there has been a shift from ethno-nationalism to more civic and benign forms of identification with the democratic political order.

However, a national-conservative turn in German politics and political culture, which many observers both inside and outside Germany feared would result from unification, has not materialized. Those who favour such a turn remain a small minority on the fringes of the political spectrum; their successes in occupying the public discourse, while undeniable, have been episodic. That being said, xenophobic and racist attacks have become a regular feature of daily life in Germany since 1992, and bear witness to the continuing existence of a violent/terrorist subculture of racism. Even more disconcerting than these attacks themselves are the fairly low levels of public outrage they inspire, as well as the fact that some rural areas and small towns in East Germany seem to have fallen under the hegemony of a xenophobic and authoritarian consensus.

But the broader picture of nationalism and statism in contemporary Germany looks different. If the era between 1871 and 1945 can be described as that of the closing of the German nation, the decades since 1968 – which include the cultural revolution of that epochal year – may signal its reopening. We have witnessed demographic changes to society through immigration; we have also seen the overcoming of the Cold War paradigm from the *Ostverträge* to German unification. In the past decades, nation-ness has shifted considerably toward the civic pole on the ethnic-civic continuum of nationalism.[46] The German variation of civic integration is usually conceptualized as *Verfassungspatriotismus*, constitutional patriotism, a term coined in the 1970s by the late Dolf Sternberger[47] and popularized by Jürgen Habermas[48] in the late 1980s. According to Sternberger's elaboration of the concept, constitutional patriotism has sought to substitute the ethno-cultural tradition of political identification, delegitimized by the Nazis and damaged by postwar division, with a shared pride in the normative framework of the *Grundgesetz* (Basic Law): 'Our national sentiment remains wounded; we do not live in the whole of Germany. But we live in a constitution, in an entire constitution, and that is in itself a kind of fatherland. Everybody feels, most know it, some of course do not want to appreciate it, that here the wind of freedom is blowing. One only has to understand that there is no freedom without state.'[49]

While *Verfassungspatriotismus* certainly sounds more civic than group identification by means of descent, it also has obviously statist overtones. The Basic Law of 1949 did not emerge from a revolution, and it has never been subjected to a referendum. It did not depend on any kind of collective action of the citizenry; rather, it was the product of the defeat of the Third Reich, Allied advice and authority, and the wisdom of the Fathers and the few Mothers of the *Grundgesetz*. The citizenry did not constitute itself in 1949; rather, it was constituted in and by the constitution. Habermas tried to rid the concept of its governmental implications by reinterpreting it as the particular pinning down of emphatically universalistic democratic norms to form what he called a 'posttraditional' (i.e., postnational) identity. This move reframed constitutional patriotism in a less statist and more civic manner by making the citizens the bearers of democratic life and practice within a deliberation-enhancing constitutional framework; yet it could hardly alter the fact that German democracy lacked a founding act to anchor this posttraditional identity.

Initial hopes that the fall of the Berlin Wall – framed as a *'nachholende Revolution,'* a revolutionary catching up[50] – could provide *post factum* for a suitable founding myth of German democracy were soon disappointed. The politics of German unification deliberately refused to make use of the symbolic capital that the Ninth of November might have provided. In particular, the absorption of the GDR into the FRG via Article 23 of the Basic Law avoided any symbolics of a founding or refounding of German democracy;[51] instead, it framed unification as a plain and simple matter of enlarging the old Federal Republic to include the five new *Länder* (states). The relocation of government and Parliament to Berlin was to be the only major symbolic concession to the epochal character of the transformation of 1989–90.

On the surface, the politics of ostentatious standstill with respect to matters of nation-ness and statism prevailed until 1998. Beneath, however, German political culture has been adapting to changing contexts. On the one hand, the ethno-national rationale has come more and more into conflict with the everyday experience of a diversifying society. On the other hand, globalization and European integration have helped demystify the state by demonstrating its dwindling regulatory and redistributive capacities. The introduction of a European citizenship in the Maastricht Treaty of 1992, the German citizenship reform of 1999, and the efforts to define a German immigration policy since 2000 – a first in a country that persistently has defined itself as being *not* a country of immigration – are manifestations of institutional and legal adjustments to changing social conditions. The struggle over citizenship reform, noted at the beginning of this article and the contentious politics of xenophobia, which made national news on a regular basis throughout the 1990s, testify to the obstinacy of the mythology of nation and state. Whether the tension between cultural disposition and social reality will be resolved by cultural change, or whether will breed a stubborn backlash against changing social conditions, a desperate clinging to categories that have lost their social reference, is an open question.

NOTES

1 See Jürgen Habermas, 'Citizenship and National Identity,' in Ronald Beiner, ed., *Theorizing Citizenship* (Albany: State University of New York Press, 1995); Claus Leggewie, 'Ethnizität, Nationalismus und multi-

kulturelle Gesellschaft,' in Helmut Berding, ed., *Nationales Bewußtsein und kollektive Identität: Studien zur Entwicklung des kollektiven Bewußtseins in der Neuzeit, vol. 2* (Frankfurt am Main.: Suhrkamp, 1994), 46–65; Henry Ashby Turner, Jr, 'Deutsches Staatsbürgerrecht und der Mythos der ethnischen Nation,' in Manfred Hettling and Paul Nolte, eds., *Nation und Gesellschaft in Deutschland: Historische Essays* (Munich: C.H. Beck, 1996), 142–50.

2 Rogers Brubaker, *Citizenship and Nationhood in France and Germany* (Cambridge: Harvard University Press, 1992), 114–19; Markus Lang, *Grundkonzeption und Entwicklung des deutschen Staatsangehörigkeitsrechts* (Frankfurt am Main.: Verlag für Standesamtswesen, 1990), 47–9.

3 On statism, citizenship, and loyalty in Germany, see Gregg O. Kvistad, *The Rise and Demise of German Statism: Loyalty and Political Membership* (New York and Oxford: Berghahn, 1999).

4 Another very important change with respect to naturalization procedures had already been made in 1992, when the older principle of legal *eligibility* to naturalization, which had left the ultimate decision to the discretion of the bureaucracy, was replaced by the principle of a legal *claim* to naturalization.

5 Statistics in this paragraph from Europäisches Forum für Migrationsstudien, Migration und Integration in Zahlen (Bamberg, 1997, available on CD-ROM, as hardcopy, and on the Web under www.uni-bamberg.de/efms), 18, 60, 91.

6 See 'Gesetz zur Reform des Staatsangehoerigkeitsrechts,' *Bundesgesetzblatt* Teil I 1999, no. 38, 23 July 1999, 1618.

7 Note that the concepts of 'organic' and 'mechanic' solidarity are applied here in the sense that dominated contemporary discourse and later became the organizing principle of Tönnies' differentiation between *Gemeinschaft* (community) and *Gesellschaft* (society), which is the *inverse* of the way Durkheim famously applies the same terminology. See Ferdinand Tönnies, *Gemeinschaft und Gesellschaft: Abhandlung des Communismus und des Socialismus als empirischer Culturformen* (Leipzig: Fues, 1887); Emile Durkheim, *De la division du travail social. Etude sur l'organisation des sociétés supérieur*, 4th ed. (Paris: F. Alcan, 1922).

8 Ernest Gellner, *Nations and Nationalism* (Ithaca: Cornell University Press, 1983), 1–7.

9 Giessen Bernhard, *Die Intellektuellen und die Nation: Eine deutsche Achsenzeit* (Frankfurt am Main: Suhrkamp, 1993), 129 (my translation).

10 Ibid. (my translation).

11 Georg W.F. Hegel, *Lectures on the Philosophy of History*, translated by J. Sibree (London: Henry G. Bohn, 1857), 466. I changed Sibree's translation

in two instances, in order to better retain the powerful, metaphoric language of Hegel's text. Sibree translates 'dass der Mensch sich auf den Kopf, d.i. auf den Gedanken stellt' as 'that man's existence centers in his head, i.e. in Thought,' which not only abandons the spatial metaphor, but also obscures the reference point for Marx's famous demand that Hegel had to be turned 'vom Kopf auf die Füße.' Also, I replaced Sibree's 'a glorious mental dawn' with 'a glorious sunrise.' The original has it as 'ein herrlicher Sonnenaufgang.' For the original text see G.W.F. Hegel, *Vorlesungen über die Philosophie der Geschichte. Werke 12* (newly edited on the basis of the *Werke* of 1832–45 by Eva Moldenhauer and Karl M. Michel) (Frankfurt am Main: Suhrkamp, 1986), 529.

12 August L. von Schlözer, *Allgemeines Staatsrecht* (Göttingen, [1793] 1970), quoted according to Hans-Ulrich Wehler, *Deutsche Gesellschaftsgeschichte. Erster Band: Vom Feudalismus des Alten Reiches bis zur Defensiven Modernisierung der Reformära, 1700–1815* (Munich: C.H. Beck, 1987), 351.

13 C.L. Reinhold, *Briefe ueber die kantische Philosophie* (Leipzig, [1790] 1923), 27, quoted according to Wehler, *Deutsche Gesellschaftsgeschichte I*, 352. See also Rudolf Vierhaus, '"Sie und nicht wir" – Deutsche Urteile über den Ausbruch der französischen Revolution,' in Jürgen Voss, ed., *Deutschland und die Französische Revolution* (Munich: Artemis, 1983), 1–15.

14 Wehler, *Deutsche Gesellschaftsgeschichte I*, 353–62.

15 Manfred Frank, *Kaltes Herz, Unendliche Fahrt, Neue Mythologie: Motiv-Untersuchungen zur Pathogenese der Moderne* (Frankfurt am Main: Suhrkamp, 1989), 93–118.

16 Reprinted in Manfred Frank and G. Kurz, eds, *Materialien zu Schellings philosophischen Anfängen* (Frankfurt am Main: Suhrkamp, 1975).

17 Ibid., 110 (my translation). It should be noted that the state the quote refers to is the state as constituted by the French Revolution.

18 The priority of synthetic over analytical operations explains why the Romantic movement is a movement of the humanities, not one of the sciences.

19 Quoted according to Dietz Bering, 'Jews and the German Language,' in Norbert Finzsch and Dietmar Schirmer, eds., *Identity and Intolerance: Nationalism, Racism, and Xenophobia in Germany and the United States* (New York and Cambridge: Cambridge University Press, 1998), 251–91, 256–7.

20 Ludwig Uhland, *Geschichte der altdeutschen Poesie: Vorlesungen an der Universität Tübingen gehalten in den Jahren 1830–1831*, 1. Theil. (Stuttgart: Cotta, 1865).

21 See Johann G. Herder, *Ideen zur Philosophie der Geschichte der Menschheit* (Wiesbaden: Fourier Verlag, 1985), 233.

22 Johann Gottlieb Fichte, *Addresses to the German Nation*, ed. with an introduction by G.A. Kelly (New York: Harper and Row, 1968), 225–6.

23 Own translation.

24 For a broader explication see Ute Gerhard and Jürgen Link, 'Zum Anteil der Kollektivsymbolik an den Nationalstereotypen,' in Jürgen Link and Wulf Wülfing, eds., *Nationale Mythen und Symbole in der zweiten Hälfte des 19. Jahrhunderts: Strukturen und Funktionen von Konzepten nationaler Identität* (Stuttgart: Klett-Cotta, 1991), 16–52.

25 See for example Hagen Schulze, *Staat und Nation in der europäischen Geschichte* (Munich: C.H. Beck, 1999), 108–49.

26 The statism argument is employed most forcefully in Gregg O. Kvistad, *The Rise and Demise of German Statism*.

27 Georg Wilhelm Friedrich Hegel, *The Philosophy of Right*, translated by T.M. Knox (Chicago: William Brenton, 1952), 80.

28 See Adam Müller, 'Von der politischen Freiheit,' in *Gesammelte Schriften I* (Munich, 1839). Quoted in Gerhard Stenzel, ed., *Die Deutschen Romantiker in vier Bänden. Bd. 1* (Salzburg: Das Bergland-Buch, 1986), 446 (my translation).

29 Gregg O. Kvistad, 'Segmented Politics: Xenophobia, Citizenship, and Political Loyalty in Germany,' in Finzsch and Schirmer, *Identity and Intolerance*, 43–70, 48–54; Kvistad, *The Rise and Demise of German Statism*, 27–54.

30 It took Prussia until 1842 to develop and institutionalize, in the Prussian Law on Subjecthood (*Preussisches Untertanengesetz*), the distinction between residents and nationals. See Lang, *Grundkonzeption des deutschen Staatsangehörigkeitsrechts*, 39; Matthias Lichter and Hoffmann Werner, *Staatsangehörigkeitsrecht*, 3rd ed. (Cologne: Heymann, 1966), 721.

31 Rudolf Vierhaus, 'Liberalismus, Beamtenstand und konstitutionelles System,' in Wolfgang Schieder, ed., *Liberalismus in der Gesellschaft des deutschen Vormärz* (Göttingen: Vandenhoeck & Ruprecht, 1983), 39–54. See also Hans-Ulrich Wehler, *Deutsche Gesellschaftsgeschichte. Zweiter Band: Von der Reformära bis zur industriellen und politischen 'Deutschen Doppelrevolution' 1815–1848/49* (Munich: C.H. Beck, 1987), 413–31.

32 Ludwig von Gerlach, in *Kreuzzeitungsrundschau*, Juli 1848, quoted in Hans-Joachim Schoeps, *Das andere Preussen*, 5th ed. (Berlin: Haude & Spener, 1981), 46 (my translation).

33 See Miroslav Hroch, *Social Preconditions of National Revival in Europe: A Comparative Analysis of the Social Composition of Patriotic Groups among the Smaller European Nations* (Cambridge: Cambridge University Press, 1985), 22–4.

34 According to Düding, the Hambacher Fest of 1832, a liberal mass rally for

national unification, already attracted a crowd of 25,000. On the eve of the 1848 revolution, the nationalist gymnastics and singing movements were organized in about 1,250 leagues with an estimated 200,000 active members. Dieter Düding, 'Die deutsche Nationalbewegung im 19. Jahrhundert: Ein Porträt ihrer Physiognomie,' in Peter Krüger, ed., *Deutschland, deutscher Staat, deutsche Nation: Historische Erkundungen eines Spannungsverhältnisses* (Marburg: Hitzeroth, 1993), 71–84, 77–9.

35 This process was driven by a variety of new media such as the increasingly popular single-volume encyclopedia and anthologies, which were instrumental in defining national treasures of knowledge and literature, and the increasing circulation of newspapers. See Wulf Wülfing, Karin Bruns, and Rolf Parr, *Historische Mythologie der Deutschen 1789–1918* (Munich: Wilhelm Fink Verlag, 1991), 14–17, 96–7.

36 Jacob Grimm, untitled preface, in Jacob Grimm and Wilhelm Grimm, *Deutsches Wörterbuch: Erster Band* (Leipzig: Verlag von S. Hirzel, 1854), lxviii (my translation).

37 Wolfgang J. Mommsen: 'The Prussian Conception of the State and the German Idea of the Empire,' in Mommsen, *Imperial Germany, 1867–1918: Politics, Culture, and Society in an Authoritarian State* (London and New York: Arnold, 1995), 41–56.

38 Wolfgang J. Mommsen, 'Nationalität im Zeichen offensiver Weltpolitik: Das Reichs- und Staatsangehörigkeitsgesetz vom 22. Juni 1913,' in Manfred Nettling and Paul Nolte, eds., *Nation und Gesellschaft in Deutschland: Historische Essays* (Munich: C.H. Beck, 1996), 128–41, 132–3.

39 Ibid., 130 (my translation).

40 Magnus Frhr. v. Braun, 'Geleitwort,' in Rudolf Klatt: *Ostpreußen unter dem Reichskommissariat 1919–1920* (Heidelberg: Quelle & Mayer, 1958), quoted in Hagen Schulze, *Weimar: Deutschland 1917–1933* (Die Deutschen und ihre Nation, Bd. 4), (Berlin: Siedler Verlag, 1982), 107 (my translation).

41 See Bernd Wunder, *Geschichte der Bürokratie in Deutschland* (Frankfurt am Main: Suhrkamp, 1986), 139–40.

42 Roland Freisler, 'Anchoring the Civil Service in the Nation,' in *Kalender für Reichsjustizbeamte* (Berlin: R. von Deckers Verlag and G. Schenck, 1938), 17–18, quoted in George L. Mosse, *Nazi Culture: A Documentary History* (New York: Schocken Books, 1966), 338 (emphasis added).

43 Wilhelm Stuckart and Hans Globke, *Kommentare zur deutschen Rassengesetzgebung*, 1(3), quoted in Mosse, *Nazi Culture*, 336.

44 Wunder, *Geschichte der Bürokratie*, 149–67. On the particular issue of the liquidation of de-Nazification, as far as the corps of civil servants is concerned, see Norbert Frei, *Vergangenheitspolitik: Die Anfänge der Bundes-*

republik und die NS-Vergangenheit (Munich: Deutscher Taschenbuchverlag, 1999), 69–99.

45 The naturalization law of 1991 removed 'positive demonstration of an attachment' to German culture from the catalogue of conditions for eligibility for naturalization; an amendment of 1992 finally granted, under certain formal conditions, a legal claim to naturalization and thus practically eliminated the discretion of the state bureaucracy (Kvistad, 'Segmented Politics,' 56). However, the expected increase in naturalizations did not materialize.

46 See for example Klaus v. Beyme, 'Deutsche Identität zwischen Nationalismus und Verfassungspatriotismus,' in Hettling/Nolte, *Nation und Gesellschaft*, 80–99; Bettina Westle, 'Traditionalismus, Verfassungspatriotismus und Postnationalismus im vereinigten Deutschland,' in Oskar Niedermayer and Klaus von Beyme, *Politische Kultur in Ost- und Westdeutschland* (Opladen: Leske & Budrich, 1996), 43–76.

47 Dolf Sternberger, 'Verfassungspatriotismus,' in *Frankfurter Allgemeine Zeitung*, 23 May 1979 (reprint in Sternberger, *Verfassungspatriotismus. Schriften X* (Frankfurt am Main: Suhrkamp, 1990), 13–16), from here on quoted as 'Verfassungsptriotismus I,' and Sternberger, 'Verfassungspatriotismus. Rede bei der 25-Jahr-Feier der "Akademie für Politische Bildung"' (1982) in Sternberger, *Verfassungspatriotismus. Schriften X*, 17–31.

48 Jürgen Habermas, *Eine Art Schadensabwicklung. Kleine politische Schriften VI* (Frankfurt am Main: Suhrkamp, 1987) 135, 173–4; Habermas, 'Die postnationale Konstellation und die Zukunft der Demokratie,' in Habermas, *Die postnationale Konstellation: Politische Essays* (Frankfurt am Main: Suhrkamp, 1998), 91–169, 116. 49 Sternberger, *Verfassungspatriotismus I*, 13 (my translation).

50 See Jürgen Habermas, *Die nachholende Revolution. Kleine politische Schriften VII* (Frankfurt am Main: Suhrkamp, 1990), 147–224.

51 Article 23 defines the area within which the Basic Law was to be operative. In the first sentence it lists the *Länder* that were part of the Federal Republic in 1949 (i.e., all West German *Länder* with the exception of the Saarland, which joined the FRG only after a referendum in 1957). The second sentence, 'In other parts of Germany, [the Basic Law] shall be put into effect after their accession,' was exclusively geared toward the eventual solution of the Saar problem. It was never intended to cover the case of unification. For this case, the preamble of the Basic Law, which was consciously drafted as a tempory arrangement, designated that a new constitution should be given: 'The entire German people remains called on completing Germany's unity and freedom in self-determination.'

Quasi a Nation: Italy's Mezzogiorno before 1848

MARTA PETRUSEWICZ

The story of modern Italy usually begins with the magic date of 1861, when Italy was 'made' and the *Risorgimento*, the movement of resurgence, triumphed. The old kingdoms, duchies, and regions that for centuries had constituted the peninsula were all dissolved and annexed to the feisty little kingdom of Piedmont-Sardinia. Austria, the villain of the previous hundred years, was defeated and forced to surrender Lombardy and all her influence on the peninsula. Venetia and Rome would follow suit. The King of Sardinia was crowned Victor Emanuel II of Italy, and an instant pantheon of founding fathers was established – Camillo Benso di Cavour, the diplomat; Giuseppe Garibaldi, the soldier; and Giuseppe Mazzini, the prophet.

Unified Italy was proclaimed reborn, as if an unspecified national unity had been lost at an equally unspecified moment in history (the Roman Empire?). *Risorgimento* became an instant catch-all term denoting an entire period in modern history, from 1800 on, during which the Italian nation struggled heroically for unity, statehood and self-determination. Even before the Italians were made (to paraphrase Massimo d'Azeglio's famous *dictum*), the myth of the Italian 'nation' was enshrined.

This development had several profound consequences. First, it bestowed on the 'Italian nation' an imperative of existence, thereby depriving any other potential imagined community on the peninsula of any right to a 'national' claim, past, present, or future. Second, it attributed sacred qualities to unity and unification, thus ruling out or stigmatizing all diversity, local specificity, and difference.

In general, this was not an ideal approach to binding together the diverse political entities that made Italy, each of them itself bestowed with a wealth of centuries-old traditions. But it turned out to be especially unfavourable, even punitive, for the southern component of the new state, the former Kingdom of Two Sicilies, which became known as the *Mezzogiorno* – the South, or noon, or meridian.

What is Italy's Mezzogiorno? The name itself evokes backwardness, poverty, and illegality. However, as a concept it lacks specificity – Mezzogiorno is simply a synonym for the South, which in turn serves as the *other* of the North. The North stands for urbanization and industrialization; the South stands for peasant civilization. The North is seen as a producer of machines, manufactured goods, services, and know-how utilizing skilled and unionized labour; the South is a producer of foodstuffs and raw materials and a supplier of cheap and docile labour. The North of the Longobard tradition (named after the long-bearded, *longa barba*, sixth-century Scandinavian conquerors) belongs to Western Europe; the South stands for the Mediterranean civilization of the Greeks and Arabs. The North is represented through its civic architecture; the South is symbolized by the permanently erupting Vesuvius. The North signifies reason, the South, passion. And so on.

This relation of *alterity* is obviously symmetrical and provides both the Mezzogiorno and the North with an identity. But in this case all the negative charges of the alterity are turned against the Mezzogiorno. Scholars, politicians, and the media – both progressive and conservative – describe the Mezzogiorno with a limited number of clearly recognizable terms of *absence, insufficiency, retardation, failure, missed opportunities, peculiarities,* and *extraordinariness*: structural economic backwardness; a wrong relationship with the state, characterized either by scarcity or by excess; a feudal or semifeudal society with no modern middle class and no Weberian 'spirits' of association, enterprise, or cooperation; and a culture that lacks rationality. They see the region as a world of anthropological peculiarities such as familism (always amoral), individualism (always possessive), factionalism, clientelism, a widespread and deeply corrupt patronage system, and an innate propensity to crime. As a society inclined to primitive rebellion but incapable of organizing for a *true* class struggle.[1] Recently, a quasi-secessionist Northern League, founded by the flamboyant Umberto Bossi, showed surprising electoral strength based mainly on its anti-Southern discourse.

Despite its lack of specificity, the Mezzogiorno is probably one of the most powerful and long-lasting representations in modern Italian history, rich in political and symbolic implications. It is Italy's *Questione Meridionale*, its 'Southern Problem.' It is narrated as a failure, or a *mancanza* – a term favoured by modern Italian intellectual tradition, which refers to occasions missed, things that might have happened and did not – which in turn causes other failures, and climaxes in the failure of Italy as a historical project. Thus, ultimately, the Mezzogiorno plays the role of Italy's negative myth of foundation, a *nazione mancata*, a nation that did not happen. It is enough to recall the sacred quality attributed to 'unity' and 'unification' since 1861 to understand why the 'Southern Problem' continues to cause so much political havoc and why the Mezzogiorno is ultimately blamed for undermining national unity. Still, what this national unity is supposed to consist of remains unclear. Not surprisingly, this question has only very recently begun to occupy historians.[2]

I

How the Mezzogiorno became a *questione*, when and by whose agency, is a matter of ongoing debate. Conventional wisdom has it that both the alterity and its specific lexicon came into being after 1861, when the unification of the country revealed an 'objective' reality hitherto hidden. The extension of free markets unveiled the structural backwardness of Southern economy; the brigandage showed the primitiveness of Southern culture; and the first socio-economic inquiries of Franchetti and Sonnino thematized the societal bases of the above.[3] Recently, more scholars have been attempting to deconstruct the representation of the Mezzogiorno and to understand the cultural sources and social needs it satisfied.[4] One of the questions raised is that of the authorship of the Southern Question: Who created the global negative image of the Mezzogiorno, using Dantesque language and medical terms and employing images of barbarity and primitiveness? Was it the *oeuvre* of the Northerners, an outcome of the civilizational clash produced by the unification? Or was it the bitter work of the Southern intelligentsia itself, elaborated in the preceding decade and ready to be adopted by the time of the unification?[5]

No doubt, the behaviour of the Southern intelligentsia at the time of the unification is a puzzle. How can we explain why a group of prominent intellectuals, courageous activists and patriots, who had endured prison and exile, remained silent or sided with the Piedmontese, even when the ethnocentricity of the new state's policies vis-à-vis the South was at its most blatant? Some scholars, following Benedetto Croce and Antonio Gramsci, attribute this behaviour to the cultural subalternity of this group, which was subservient to the landowning class and developed in the shadow of the *feudo*. Others argue that in ten years of exile, the expatriates discovered the cultural and political superiority of the North. Still others, including this author, think that the silence of the *ceto civile* – the civic-minded and practice-oriented intelligentsia, who will be discussed further – was a defection, the fruit of a bitter disenchantment after the defeat of the 1848 revolution.

In this paper I propose to explore further this story of hope, disenchantment, and defection by examining the character, ideas, and social practices of the Southern *ceto civile* in the half-century preceding 1848. I will show how passionately this group had been involved in a political and cultural modernization of their country, how enthusiastically they had greeted in 1848 the fulfilment of their work, and how bitter they felt when they saw all this betrayed and defeated in 1849. Furthermore, and more importantly, I will argue that this involvement amounted to a mature and conscious political project, which might have led to the construction of a Neapolitan nation and the transformation of their country into a modern nation-state.

Two preliminary remarks. The first is that such an attempt was not at all extraordinary in the context of the nineteenth century. As Eric Hobsbawm has reminded us, there was nothing inevitable about the number of nations that emerged; there existed a number of 'possible' nations that never materialized, though endowed with all the nation-making material. The Neapolitan nation certainly fell into this category.[6] The second is that the possible emergence of such a nation was not in contradiction with the cultural identity of Neapolitan elites, which was and had long been Italian and rooted in high culture, classical education, and the Italian language. The problem is that the Risorgimento rhetoric has accustomed us to consider this idea of national identity – composed of language, culture, religion, and a shared ethical and spiritual heritage – as the only basis for constructing a national community. In reality, as Benedict Anderson has shown, this 'old' identity can coexist in a national elite with a new modern identity, constructed around the notion of citizenship and engaged in inventing new traditions. The Southern elite was building up both identities, whose *loci* did not correspond: they shared the Italian discourse with a small and culturally homogenous minority of the population of over 20 million, while the Neapolitan project was to eventually involve 8 million inhabitants to be made into citizens. Of these two identities, it is the latter, the modern one, that will occupy us in these pages.

II

The 'prerequisites' for, or the ingredients of, a Neapolitan national community had been in place since the mid-eighteenth century: a modern sovereign state endowed with a rational bureaucratic structure; a stable *national* dynasty; clearly established and uncontested borders; and a widely accepted political monarchical order. There was also choice available in myth-making material: from the freedom-loving ancient Brutii, Catoni, and Enotri, to the *polis*, trade, and philosophy of the Magna Grecia, to Frederick II's thirteenth-century 'modern' medieval state.[7] Some could even detect a Neapolitan cultural identity, one that combined the quintessentially *rational* character of the culture with the *genius loci* derived from the landscape and popularized by the Romantics. There were founding fathers – the eighteenth-century intellectual giants such as Giambattista Vico, Pietro Giannone, and Antonio Genovesi, and the luminaries of the Enlightenment. And there were the martyrs of 1799.

The actual realization of the modern nation-making project would involve three components: the modernization of the state, the growth of the middle class, and the emancipation of the people (*popolo*). The first required full sovereignty (thus the great symbolic importance of the conflict with the papacy in the 1770s and 1780s), but also political liberalization in the direction of a constitutional monarchy. The second demanded the extension of civil society and the consolidation of a national elite as a repository of the secular and critical consciousness of the nation. The last meant improving the social conditions of the peasantry and a far-reaching program of education aimed at transforming the brutish and ignorant *plebe* into a citizenship-deserving *popolo*.

The emerging *ceto civile* constituted a national elite, one that was to play the central role in the nation-building project. Besides being the project's initiator and main vehicle, the *ceto civile* also served as a bridge between the other two components, negotiating with the dynasty on the one end and the peasantry on the other, proposing political and social reforms, and acting as the advocate for the people. The *ceto civile* escapes a precise definition; it was a sort of a practice-oriented intelligentsia composed of civil servants, technical experts, and lawyers. Strong supporters of Neapolitan autonomy since the seventeenth century, it was they who bore responsibility for the state in the last phases of Spanish rule. In the process, they gained self-confidence and consolidated their idea of autonomy, which acquired social and economic content and emerged as a truly civil conception of the Neapolitan nation-state. For this conception, the *ceto civile* claimed natural leadership.[8] Among these eighteenth-century 'fathers of the nation,' the writer Pietro Giannone was the most influential in shaping conceptions of national identity. Eleonora de Fonseca Pimentel – poet, journalist, and political activist, one of the 'martyrs' executed in 1799 – credited Giannone, the author of *Istoria civile del regno di Napoli*, with making the Neapolitans into an (almost) new nation, *'quasi una nuova Nazione.'*[9] Giannone's concept of national identity was built on freedom, social consensus, and liberal government; the sovereignty of the state would necessarily be accompanied by some form of a social contract, which would guarantee the nation's rights. All of this required, and was almost identical to, a modernization project: it had to start with a radical critique of the existing laws and institutions and continue with a far-reaching program of legal, political, administrative, economic, and social reforms.

The preconditions for modern nation making had been developing since the mid-eighteenth century. In 1734 the Neapolitan kingdom achieved independence from Spain and became the largest of the Italian states. It was governed on a stable basis by one dynasty, a branch of the Bourbons, which was rapidly 'neapolitanized.' Although still in the Spanish orbit, the kingdom developed an autonomous foreign policy, the strength of which was especially relevant in relation to the papacy. Vast commercial opportunities were opened to it. Independence and a strong recovery from the long seventeenth-century crisis propelled efforts to improve the country's material conditions. Don Carlos and his son Ferdinand attempted far-reaching reforms aimed at restricting feudal privilege, reforming finances and taxation, reorganizing the prison system, and reducing the Catholic Church's wealth and power. They created a modern land registry (*cadastre*), reorganized the system of grain reserves (*annona*), negotiated an accord with the Church, and expelled the Jesuits. The year 1783 saw the establishment of the *Cassa Sacra*, a form of national land trust whose purpose was to oversee (mainly) expropriated ecclesiastic property. At this point a radical land reform was attempted; this involved expropriating and redistributing the Church's wealth and curtailing baronial privileges. Don Carlos and Ferdinand patronized culture, built the splendid San Carlo theatre, and sponsored the first archeological excavations at Herculaneum and Paestum.

Ferdinand sought the intellectuals' approval and support, and under his patronage the intelligentsia thrived. The ailing University of Naples was revived, and the first chair of political economy in continental Europe was established there. The position was first held by the noted economist Antonio Genovesi. The writings and the teachings of intellectual giants such as Genovesi, Galanti, Carlo Antonio Broggia, Ferdinando Galiani, and Giuseppe Palmieri made the Neapolitan Enlightenment famous throughout Europe. The inspirational teachings of the masters, combined with the opportunity to put those teachings into practice through the king's reform projects, triggered a movement of moral and institutional innovation and activism. A new intelligentsia was emerging that was concerned about the public good and capable of political agency. These men constituted Fonseca Pimentel's 'almost a new nation' composed of *philosophes* and their pupils, joined by many elements of the nobility, the clergy, and the ever-present legal professionals (the *legulei*). But at the same time, as noted philosopher and historian Benedetto Croce pointed out, many people were excluded: the multitudinous *plebe* of the capital city – the little people (*popolo minuto*) consisting of artisans, servants, and courtiers – and the peasants and shepherds living outside Naples. In other words, most of the kingdom's population. Furthermore, the newly forming bourgeoisie chose not to join, since they were too busy making money to involve themselves in public affairs. Nevertheless, a new elite was emerging – one that was both well educated and representative, as well as capable of assuming political agency. The new institution of freemasonry provided this elite with both cohesion and an attractive 'religion' of reason and humanity. A 'national' language of patriotism (*patria*) and love of the nation (*amor di patria*) was gaining ascendancy. The patriotic activities of the new elite were profoundly different from the municipalist boasting and rivalries of the past.[10]

The new elite was faithful to Giannone's idea of nation building. Precisely *because* its members cared about the public good and the future of the *patria*, it was relentless in its critique of the kingdom's backwardness and of the conditions that were impeding the country's progress. In the many works representative of this critique, we find a detailed indictment of the institutions and customs of the feudal system, of the iniquitous tax regime, which discriminated against the entrepreneurial and labouring classes, of the aristocrats' powers, of the unbalanced land tenure system, and of the peasants' abject poverty.

By the end of the eighteenth century the Neapolitan quasi-nation was entering its political adolescence.[11] Around the same time, the political context was rapidly changing. With the French Revolution and the execution of Louis XVI, the unspoken pact between the Neapolitan intellectuals and the dynasty came to an end: reforms were abandoned and even reversed, and intellectuals were ostracized and persecuted. The years 1799 to 1815 were turbulent ones marked by revolution, civil war, foreign rule, and a series of military defeats. The quasi-nation joined the revolution in 1799, supported the short-lived Partenopean Republic, and fell victim to the counter-revolutionary mob's rage and to Ferdinand's cruel vengeance. In 1806 it offered its support to the French kings (Joseph and then Murat) installed in Naples by Napoleon's troops, and backed them in their efforts to modernize the state and society. After the 'Napoleonic decade' came to an end in 1815, the Neapolitan monarchy was restored.

Though absolutist, the restoration regime was different from the *ancien régime* in that the Bourbons did not attempt to restore feudalism and maintained most of the administrative and institutional reforms made by Murat. Freedom of the press was generally upheld, notwithstanding periods of aggressive censorship. Ferdinand I turned reactionary, but he was not a fanatic: he favoured some degree of modernization, though he was against the constitutional reforms attempted in the revolution of 1820. His son Francis I's reign was uneventful. Hope rose again in 1830, when Ferdinand II came to the throne. As one of Europe's new cohort of activist but also absolutist monarchs, he seemed committed to modernizing the Neapolitan state and society. He granted amnesty to the kingdom's exiles and asked them to return. Although adamantly opposed to representative government, he carried out a true administrative revolution; he also encouraged the development of industry and banking and initiated the construction of railways.[12]

The Neapolitan quasi-nation did not fall into languor and desolation; quite the contrary – having been restored, it set energetically to work. The past twenty years had helped clarify its modernizing project and free it from that political and intellectual shackles that had led it to surrender to Neapolitan sovereignty. Vincenzo Cuoco's analysis of the 'passivity' of the 1799 revolution well reflects the intellectual mood among the post-Napoleonic elite. They challenged their masters on a series of points: the universalism of prescriptions for economic and political development, the contempt for native customs and institutions, and the regime's remoteness from popular sentiment. The new elites found inspiration in their Neapolitan predecessor Giambattista

Vico, who had taught that societies should be taken on their own individual terms rather than in terms of universal categories. Influenced by the Romantic movement, younger intellectuals sought out local influences: traditions, economic 'vocations,' and 'spirits' of the territory (the *genii loci*). They initiated programs of local action, making use of newly formed regional associations and journals, and the abandoned freemasonry, which was falling into decline. This new emphasis on 'localism' helped mobilize the provinces; a new 'civic' space was beginning to take shape. Though it had not yet quite reached the *popolo*, the new nation was nevertheless growing.

The main point of contention with the throne remained the question of the constitution and representative government; no modern nation could exist without political participation and the extension of citizenship. This conflict unfolded through a series of promises, negotiations, and concessions. In the meantime, the modernizing elite set out to extend the bases of a nation though education and various reform projects. The goals of the new nation were to modernize the state and its governance, to reform the economic system, and to help the *plebe* evolve into a *popolo* through literacy programs, social reforms, and structural improvements.

The cultural climate was lively. Naples swarmed with students – all 'liberals' – from every part of the country. A multitude of new public and private schools, institutes, and academies thrived; many of these were run by the most illustrious members of the Neapolitan intelligentsia, such as the literary scholar Francesco De Sanctis, the economist Antonio Scialoia, the historian Francesco Trinchera, and the jurist Pasquale Stanislao Mancini. Years later, in *La giovinezza*, de Sanctis painted an extraordinary portrait of private education in Naples during that period: free, liberal, and unique. His own school was self-governing, and he compared the approach it took to the French utopian thinker Proudhon's style of anarchy: a 'small self-contained society, without rules, without discipline, without any authority of command, moved by sentiments of duty, value, and reciprocal respect.'[13] All of these schools sought out the talented provincial youth, attracting them with fellowships, free tuition, and competitive 'incentive awards.' The upper-class provincial youth had always gone to Naples to study; now, in Pasquale Villari's words, 'students were flowing in thousands,' many of them offspring of provincial gentry, lawyers, and sometimes even artisans.[14] Besides the traditional disciplines such as law, medicine, the military arts, and philosophy, the new popular fields were Italian, political economy, history, engineering, and architecture. The students were pervaded by the Romantic spirit, engrossed in Italian literature (both fantastic and sentimental), and attuned to all 'rumours' from Lombardy.

The fine arts were also thriving; artists, art students, visitors, and distinguished foreigners were flooding toward Naples. New schools and 'revolutionary' Romantics were successfully challenging the cultural authority of the classicist Academy of Fine Arts. The Royal Court was patronizing artists through exhibitions and commissions. In 1825, Francesco I instituted an annual exhibition modelled on the French salons. Private patrons followed this royal example, buying the works of art students and offering them commissions and fellowships.

The salons held in patrician houses (*case*) played a vital role in extending the borders of the new nation. The elites' patronage most evident in those houses. Many patrician families counted scholars and authors as family members; examples include *casa* De Thomasis, *casa* Poerio, and *casa* Ricciardi. Within these houses, politics was often mediated by culture. The *case* were generally liberal; the artists were liberal as well, but beholden to the regime for favours. The students were more radical; many were associated with the secret societies (*Carboneria*) and with various conspiracies. They were politically passionate, as would be made clear in 1848, when they took to the streets and the *case* intellectuals formed the parliaments and the governments.

Even in the provinces, life seemed less monotonous. The *Carbonari* – radical, anti-clerical, anti-Bourbon – were the heroes of the provincial youth, and the Romantic mood of the times was overwhelming. Young people were reading Mme de Staël, Sir Walter Scott, and Alessandro Manzoni. They wrote and published their own work in a growing number of journals: poems, ballads, plays, and novellas, but also history, folklore, *rumanze* (stories of common people's love and passion), and *impressioni* (impressionistic *ad hoc* accounts). They also wrote about archeology, philosophy, and psychology. There was a great deal of theatre, with a long opera season and a shorter drama season. Young members of the elite travelled in Italy and throughout Europe; during these *Bildung* tours they met exiles, political activists, and foreign and Italian intellectuals and artists.

The young often involved themselves in conspiracies, which sometimes led to imprisonment and even execution. Yet this sort of repression was neither continuous nor universal. In 'normal' times there was room to express ideas and opinions. Local and foreign journals and reviews circulated widely; new legal journals promoted the new juridical culture; and literary reviews flourished. Every association and professional organization, and every political or literary movement, published some sort of periodical. One of the most influential journals, *Il Progresso delle scienze, delle lettere, delle arti*, was founded in 1832 and edited for some time by Giuseppe Ricciardi. Liberal and pluralistic, it favoured a diversity of approaches; it accommodated four political generations and political views, ranging from the radical republicanism of Ricciardi to the conservative municipalism of Luigi Blanch. There were also several left-wing journals: republican, radical, democratic, and anticapitalist.

There was a broad and general interest in things economic, as reflected in the success of journals such as *Il Gran Sasso d'Italia*, founded and directed by Ignazio Rozzi, agronomist and professor of agriculture in Abruzzi; *Annali della Calabria Citeriore*, founded and directed in Cosenza by Luigi Maria Greco, a sharp conservative social critic; and *Giornale di Statistica*, one of the first reviews of statistics in Europe, founded in 1835 in Palermo by two young brilliant liberal economists, Francesco Ferrara and Emerico Amari. It is interesting that even establishment-sponsored publications – for example, the governmental organ *Giornale del Regno delle Due Sicilie* – were often critical of the very institutions that published them. The most important was the *Annali civili del Regno delle Due Sicilie*, founded in 1833 by a group of young journalists close to the established reformist circles. The *Annali* counted among its collaborators some of the best and most influential writers, civil servants, and administrators of the period, and it coordinated the efforts of various economic and cultural associations. Even some members of the clergy became vehicles of the nation-making project. Many provincial priests were active members of economic societies, contributors to economic journals, teachers in agrarian academies and schools, and strong promoters of innovation and agrarian improvement. Some seminaries established schools of practical agronomy for the peasantry.

Probably the most important vehicle of the nation-making discourse was the new associationism, which was radically different from the tradition of secret societies and freemasonry. In this vein, special attention should be paid to economic societies, both because their reach was so long and because they transformed government instruments into autonomous loci of critical discourse. The kingdom's economic societies – fourteen on the continent and a few more in Sicily – constituted the largest network of their kind on the Italian peninsula. They gathered and disseminated information and statistics; promoted new technology and experimentation; stimulated innovation and rationalization through exhibits, fairs, competitions, and awards; encouraged vocational and general education by establishing various levels of agricultural schools, as well as model teaching farms and experimental gardens; and established scholarships for poor students. This network involved several thousand people, but its influence was broader still. In smaller towns, their meetings (*comizi*) brought together the local middle class – professionals, entrepreneurial farmers, artisans – with landowners, judges, civil servants, and university professors, thus facilitating a certain mixing of classes while disseminating the ideas of the national elite. They were also highly active in publishing: besides more than twenty journals – from annual to bimonthly, from economic to literary-agrarian – economic societies sponsored and published manuals, textbooks, almanacs, calendars, and 'agrarian catechisms.' Their target audiences ranged from barely literate peasants to small property owners to medium-size landowners engaged in specialized production.

III

A certain common discourse transpires from these different loci of civil society. Their representation of the country was, at once, pessimistic and optimistic. Having adopted the imperative of progress and the 'European' criteria of its measurement, they considered the conditions of *development* and *backwardness* not as dichotomous oppositions, but rather as different relative positions on a material and temporal continuum. Accordingly, they viewed the Two Sicilies as a backward country in comparison with those 'ahead' of it, such as England, France, the United States, Lombardy, Tuscany, and Prussia, but more or less at the same point as Ireland and ahead of Russia and Poland. Consequently, despite the many problems in the kingdom, progress was possible; they could, as Francesco Saverio Salfi put it, '*porre la nazione al livello di quelle che l'hanno sorpassata*' (bring the nation up to the level of those who surpassed her).[15]

Foremost among the nation's problems was the agrarian system, which held the entire economy back. It was wedded to antiquated crops, methods, and instruments, imprisoned by ill-defined and confused property relations, resistant to innovation, and increasingly wasteful, inefficient, and irrational. Following this on the list of problems were bad commercial policies; poor conditions for industry and manufacturing; the pitiful state of the transportation infrastructure; the absence of banks and credit institutions; and, finally, the 'social question' – that is, the general condition of the peasantry, which was characterized by poverty, poor health, insecurity of land tenure, and widespread illiteracy.

Still, some progress had been made since feudalism – the archenemy of progress – had been abolished in 1806. The country was partaking in the *Zeitgeist* of progress, so compelling at that time. It was endowed with natural resources and with a steadily growing population, and the government was moving in the right direction by building railways and factories, modernizing institutions, and loosening some tariff regulations. Further remedies were possible. Everyone agreed on the importance of education and good government. In fact, the reform of education engaged the best intellects of the period, from Vincenzo Cuoco to Francesco De Sanctis, while the 'administrative revolution' of the 1830s involved the best and most innovative legal scholars, such as Pasquale Stanislao Mancini, Matteo De Augustinis, and Giuseppe De Thomasis.

Although its backwardness was severe and catching up would require energy and effort, the kingdom's prospects were not at all bleak. Many new approaches were being found and taken. This was reflected in the artistic representations of the time; these showed a rural and traditional country, with barefoot peasants standing in front of their huts; but they also showed an industrial and modernizing nation – witness Silvano Fergola's railways, stations, and suspended iron bridges, and Giuseppe De Nittis's and Luigi Fergola's industrial landscapes with their factory chimneys.

The different loci of civil society were helping create and extend the kingdom's cultural cohesion. The quasi-nation was growing, mobilizing opinion and establishing ties with the *popolo minuto*. It was ready to reach out to the peasants; though dominated by landowners, it was nevertheless beginning to accept the imperative of a land reform. The peasantry, too, as Enrica Di Ciommo argued, was becoming less loyalist and more susceptible to revolutionary mobilization.[16] By 1848 the Neapolitan quasi-nation felt strong enough to demand a say in the country's governance.

IV

In mid-January 1848 a revolution began in Sicily, followed quickly by an uprising in Naples. Both were modern national revolutions, part of

the European wave. But whereas the Sicilian uprising had strong sepa-
ratist overtones, the Neapolitan one resembled the contemporary ur-
ban revolutions of Paris, Vienna, and Berlin – it was a revolution of the
artisans and youth, pervaded by the Romantic culture. The streets of
Naples and the barricades were manned by the pupils of De Sanctis,
Puoti, and Scialoia, who were full of ideas gleaned from Hegel,
Chateaubriand, de Staël, Lamartine, and Hugo, as well as Colletta,
Berchet, and Gioberti. It was a revolution of the intellectuals, as Lewis
Namier put it, but also a revolution of all, of the nation. 'Each honest
heart joined the festive banquet,' wrote the novelist Francesco Mastriani:
intellectuals and students, artisans and peasants, returning exiles.[17]
The atmosphere in Naples was excited, festive; with the theatres shut,
the unemployed singers sang popular and revolutionary songs in the
streets.[18] 'I always recall that Spring of 1848,' Giuseppe Sodano wrote
later. Sodano was a former monk, a writer and historian, and in 1848
served as president of the *Circolo del progresso*. 'Those unforgettable
days when we were free. That who did not see those days, never saw
anything truly great and sublime.'[19]

The revolution quickly achieved the dreams of the Neapolitan reformers; with a constitution and the two parliaments, the kingdom
finally joined the community of civilized nations. New governments
and legislatures in Naples and Palermo included many of the representatives of the quasi-nation: Carlo Poerio, Luigi Dragonetti, Antonio
Scialoia, Francesco Ferrara, the brothers Michele and Emerico Amari.
The government formed in April 1848 by historian Carlo Troya was
composed of the most respected moderate critics of the old regime,
active contributors to the nation-making discourse with years of public
experience behind them. Troya himself was a conservative, but Luigi
Dragonetti (Foreign Affairs) and jurist Raffaele Conforti (Internal Affairs) were democrats, while Paolo Emilio Imbriani (Public Education)
and Antonio Scialoia (Agriculture, Industry, and Commerce) were confirmed liberals. Although moderate, the government was sincere in its
opposition to absolutism and determined to carry out reforms. It granted
amnesty for all political offences, abolished the Ministry of Police, took
away popular education from the bishops, and opened schools in even
the smallest villages.

The prevailing mood in the continental kingdom was conciliatory
and rather moderate, with only a few republican or adamantly anti-
Bourbon voices. (Sicily's story is different, as by April the island had *de
facto* seceded.) Most agreed that a constitutional monarchy was the best

guarantee of stability and was necessary for progress; also, that the Bourbons and Ferdinand were up to this task. Even the peasant movements and land occupations were less frightening than in 1799 and certainly less hostile to the liberals. The election of 18 April 1848 confirmed the nation's commitment to the revolution, from both liberals and radicals alike.

But on 15 May the king refused to take the oath of allegiance to the constitution. The 'events' followed. But unlike in Paris in June of the same year, in Naples the 'nation' – the National Guard, the bourgeois, the students, the artisans, and the peasants – was all on one side, defending the revolution in the streets and at the barricades. The provinces rushed to the defence of Parliament, with the Calabrians conspicuous in their uniforms on the streets of Naples – the reverse of what happened in 1799. The treacherous king was standing alone.

The conciliatory mood had ended. In response to calls for an armed insurrection and for the crushing of the monarchy, Ferdinand dissolved Parliament, called new elections with limited suffrage, and arrested and expelled the radicals and the democrats. As had happened in France, the revolution was defended in many rural districts; in Calabria this resistance continued into the fall. Despite restricted suffrage, the November elections returned many revolutionaries to Parliament, confirming the nation's commitment to the revolution. Next came the 'perjury': in March 1849, Ferdinand dissolved Parliament and cancelled the constitution.

To the extent that the revolution was a test of maturity for the quasination, the result seemed positive. At the present state of research, it is impossible to say to what degree the quasi-nation had been enlarged between 1799 and 1848 or how much popular participation there was in 1848. Many of the revolution's leaders, including moderates, felt that the revolution had indeed been fought by the enlarged nation – the youth, the bourgeoisie, the intelligentsia, some of the aristocracy, some of the common people (*basso popolo*) – and that its ideas were quickly spreading among artisans and workers. A revolutionary alliance as broad as this was proof that in those fifty years the Mezzogiorno had indeed partaken fully in the European processes of political and civil growth: the liberals had shed their cultural and political dependency on France and evolved from secret societies into modern associationism, and the *plebe*, no more ignorant or superstitious than other peoples of Europe, had grown and matured and become a *popolo*. 'Those Calabrians,' wrote de Sanctis, 'who then [in 1799] shouted death to the liberals, in '48 raised the first cry of freedom in Europe.' The strength of the revolutionary alliance between the *popolo* and the intelligentsia had forced Ferdinand to make concessions: 'That cry of the few had an accomplice in the sentiment of an entire *popolo* ready to rise.'[20]

V

In the European context, the defeat of the Neapolitan revolution is not a surprise: both the revolution and the counter-revolution were part of a general European wave. At the beginning of 1848, no government seemed able to survive; by 1849, no uprising could. That being said, other countries that had experienced a revolution – France, Piedmont, Prussia, even Austria – upheld some of the reforms introduced in 1848. In contrast, the king of the Two Sicilies responded with vicious repression, abandoning all projects of modernization.

The repression was severe and vindictive; its tools included terror, mass arrests, intimidations, assassinations, countless trials, and long prison sentences. Generally speaking, it was less bloody and less spectacular than in 1799 – death sentences were rarely followed by executions. However, it lasted much longer and was much more widespread, with endless show trials and thousands arrested. The Ministry of the Police was re-established, and a police state was introduced. Broad networks of informers and spies were used as means to control and punish the state's adversaries. Endless checks were run on the political, religious, and moral conduct of candidates for government-related jobs. The officers of all associations were required to swear under oath that they did not and would never belong to any secret society. A mere police report was sufficient for a Neapolitan to be listed as *attendibile* (i.e., suspected of liberal inclinations), some 300,000 were, and thereby banned from the civil service and many other jobs (attorney, university professor, even the director of the Pompeii excavations). That figure represented almost half of all the literate people in the kingdom!

Not only people but also ideas and goods were subject to control. Civil and ecclesiastical authorities enacted strict censorship; prohibitive duties were placed on imported books; protective tariffs were placed on imports and exports that were far higher than the economy could possibly have required. The king had made a political choice to cut his kingdom off from the world; as one writer put it, he erected a sort of 'Great Wall of China' around his domain.

The results were predictable. Even the most cautious reforms were abandoned, public works projects were dropped, and responsibility for education was given back to the Church, which was also to provide whatever social services it deemed necessary. The general result was severe damage to civil society and to the emerging nation.

Among the victims of repression, the intelligentsia held the place of honour. The Neapolitan elite found itself in prison: radicals as well as moderate liberals, republicans as well as monarchists, members of secret societies as well as elected politicians. Huge show trials were held in Naples – for the members of *Unità italiana*, for Carlo Poerio, for the '44' with Scialoia and Spaventa, for the '40 defaulters.' Hundreds more trials, also spectacular though smaller in scale, were held in the provinces. Penalties included capital punishment (usually, however, not carried out), placing in irons, and life in prison. The horror of those prisons was immortalized by the young William Gladstone in his *Two Letters to the Earl of Aberdeen*. The repression produced more exiles than ever before in the country's history, and their numbers grew even more when some life sentences were commuted to deportation.

By the mid-1850s, significant numbers of the quasi-nation found themselves outside the borders of the country. Once abroad, some of them joined freedom struggles elsewhere. Others settled into the exile's life in Piedmont, France, Switzerland, England, or Tuscany, where they plotted, kept up their hopes, and waited for the chance to return.

Those of the intelligentsia who were not imprisoned or exiled went into 'internal exile.' Often they had no choice; once listed as *attendibili*, they were forced from public life. Yet even conservatives wanted to escape the subservience that participation in public life required. Civil society quickly collapsed: most of the journals that had flourished in the previous decades were shut by the censor or folded on their own; meetings of learned socieites became abstract and boring. Except for a few prominent intellectuals who collaborated with the throne, a few 'loyal' scholars who denounced the 'errors and fallacies of Mr. Gladstone,' and some rabid reactionaries who rejoiced at the return of the Christian order, the 'nation' stood silent or kept to neutral subjects.

As often happens, the repression seemed at first to actually consolidate the nation-making process. The regime revealed its brutal face, rendering unbridgeable the chasm between 'us' and 'them,' the 'nation' and the 'Bourbon.' Moreover, by cutting across class barriers, the repression brought together intellectuals and artisans, noblemen and peasants; '*popolani* and bourgeois locked to the same chain,' wrote De Sanctis. The intellectuals were thrilled by instances of popular resistance and by the pride expressed by the *popolani* at being called political prisoners. The show trials popularized the ideas under indictment and brought those ideas the support and admiration of other Europeans. Even the horrors of the prisons were worth bearing, when William Gladstone, after a visit to Carlo Poerio and Michele Pironti, turned them in his *Two Letters* into a powerful accusation against the Bourbon regime, 'the negation of God elevated to the method of government.' In his 1851 introduction to the Italian translation of Gladstone's *Letters*, published in Piedmont, Giuseppe Massari speaks of the 'great battle of civilization against barbarie, of reason against ignorance, of virtue against vice, of innocence against calumny.'[21] The terms of 'barbarity,' 'ignorance,' 'vice' and 'calumny' apply here exclusively to the Bourbon government; the 'great battle' is one against tyranny. The country is something different from its government; it represents civilization, reason, virtue, and innocence. Full of human and natural resources, it is inhabited by a *popolo* both strong and generous.

In the longer term, however, the effects of repression were profoundly destructive. For the third time in half a century the South was losing a significant fraction of its intelligentsia, and this time the 'blood letting' was severe and long lasting. Over the years, internal discord grew and the edifice of the quasi-nation began to crumble. Bitter and impotent, the intelligentsia waited for the *popolo* to rise and bring about the collapse of the 'rotten body of tyranny that keeps it prisoner.'[22] But the *popolo* was not rising, nor was the regime about to collapse. For years, the prisoners and exiles placed their hopes in every conspiracy, every assassination attempt, every local rebellion, hoping it would unleash a general uprising. Each time, they were disappointed. The cholera epidemics in 1854 were not followed by popular unrest, as had happened in 1837. The king, following his policy of seclusion, refused to get involved in the Crimean War. Plans for a military expedition that was to land in 1856 on the Neapolitan coast, under the command of Luciano Murat, fell through. The 1857 'action program' that Luigi Settembrini and Silvio Spaventa addressed from prison to the no better specified 'Southern parties' (*partiti meridionali*) met with no reaction. The final blow was the tragedy of Sapri in the province of Salerno, where three hundred young revolutionaries led by Carlo Pisacane were massacred by local peasants. Anger and despair were growing. In a letter from prison to his wife, Settembrini screams out his anger against 'this *popolo*, or rather this *volgo* filled with ricotta.'[23] In a significant reversal, the *popolo* once again becomes *volgo*.

Why was the *popolo* not rising? This painful question begged for a reflection on the 1848 revolution, on its strengths and shortcomings, on the realities of the liberal revolutionary alliance, and on the internal cohesion of the quasi-nation and its ties with the *popolo*. The occasion was mostly wasted, however; disappointment and resentment dominated the debates, often turning analysis into blame and recriminations.

Some *topoi* of the Mezzogiorno's future representation appear in that debate: 'Our country is a deeply infirm body, that has no vital force left to recover' writes Antonio Scialoja from prison in 1850, 'abject vices and deep corruption, for centuries the affliction of our society [...] have totally destroyed in it logic, morality and common sense.'[24] Faithful to its bleak tradition, the government encourages those evils, considering them indispensable conditions of its own existence.

The bluntest formulation of this discourse came from Francesco Trinchera – historian, hero of 1848, exile – in his 1855 pamphlet *La quistione napoletana*. The occasion was significant. Some of the intelligentsia, mostly exiles, announced their support for Luciano Murat's candidacy for the throne of Naples. Murat was the son of the former king. The idea in itself was not new; what *was* different was that support for an authoritarian solution was coming from former republicans and radicals.

The question posed by Trinchera, a committed Murattist, was: Do the Neapolitan liberals have enough strength to deliver themselves from the yoke of this 'most vicious of governments'? His answer is an emphatic no: they do not, and they never did.[25] The paralysis of Neapolitan society is the outcome not only of the symbiosis of the barbaric dynasty with the backward *plebe*, but also of the vagueness and abstraction of the day-dreaming intelligentsia. All together are responsible for the dreadful state of the country. Trinchera's language is heavy: 'brutal' and 'savage' is the government that 'tortures,' 'poisons,' and 'corrupts' an entire nation; that turns the country into a civil and institutional 'desert,' with no sign of 'civilized life, no useful institution ... no public or private education, no roads, no commerce, no industry'; a desert populated by a *popolo* that is 'degenerate,' filled with superstitions, cruel and violent, that 'delights in murder and robbery' and 'who knows no law nor God, and had long lost any notion of good and evil.' The intelligentsia is naive, its thought 'blocked' by years of 'religious and political tyranny,' 'removed from the real world,' dreamers of a government that, rooted in virtue, could never be made 'in the midst of a horde of savages.' Great individuals, the best men in the country –

educated, moral, and heroic – can do nothing against a 'despotism immobile and inflexible as the ancients' fate, which reposes over a large inert mass.'[26]

Here, despotism and the masses depend on and support each other in a toxic embrace. Has there ever been an alliance between the intelligentsia and the *popolo*? Trinchera's answer is again negative: this *popolo* is too degenerate to even understand freedom, let alone 'desire it, and die for it and with it.' There has never been any alliance; the chasm cannot be bridged.

Trinchera's pamphlet was one of many. Undoubtedly, by the late 1850s both the lexicon and all the main *topoi* of the Mezzogiorno were in place: the infirmity of a country that had lost its *elan vitale*; the centuries-long character of this condition; the degeneration and deep moral corruption of the *popolo*; its sinister symbiosis with the regime; and the unbridgeable chasm between the *popolo* and the intelligentsia. Such a viciously bitter representation played a double-role: on the one hand, it proved that there had never been a chance of winning because the project of modern nation building had been a pipe dream; on the other, it revealed that there was no future either, no autonomy, because no independent project for the South had any reason to exist. The Mezzogiorno was a failure because it had failed to make itself into a modern nation.

The consequences of the defection of the Neapolitan *ceto civile* have been weighing down Italian history ever since. The specific terms of the 'Southern Problem' shift, as do the responses of various governments, which oscillate between interventionism and indifference, but the 'Problem' remains and continues to be perceived as a 'national' one. The changing political climate of recent years may represent, however, a chance for the Mezzogiorno to liberate itself from its representation as a 'problem.' Regional autonomy is on the rise in Italy, and local governments are growing stronger, and these developments are creating conditions in which the *ceto civile* and the *popolo* of the South could grasp their own destiny and build on their own distinct traditions and cultural identity. But this is a different history, the history of the present.

NOTES

1 In the late nineteenth century, Italian sociologist and anthropologist Cesare Lombroso claimed that Southerners had an innate predisposition to crime.

See for example L'uomo delinquente: studiato in rapporto alla antropologia, alla medicina legale ed alle discipline carcerarie (Milan: Hoepli, 1876). 'A-moral familism' was a term introduced in the 1958 book The Moral Basis of a Backward Society (Chicago: Free Press, 1965) by the American anthropologist Edward Banfield; this line of interpretation has returned in Robert Putnam's Making Democracy Work: Civic Traditions in Modern Italy (Princeton, NJ: Princeton University Press, 1992). Eric J. Hobsbawm's Primitive Rebels: Studies in Archaic Forms of Social Movement in the 19th and 20th Centuries (New York: F.A. Praeger, 1963) comes from a very different perspective. For a recent English-language review of the literature of alterity, see Robert Lumley and Jonathan Morris, eds., The New History of the Italian South: Revisiting the Mezzogiorno (Edinburgh: Exeter Press, 1998); Jane Schneider, ed., Italy's Southern Question: 'Orientalism' in One Country (Oxford: Berg, 1998); and John Davis, 'Changing Perspectives on Italy's "Southern Problem"' in Carl Levy, ed., Italian Regionalism: History, Identity and Politics (Oxford: Berg, 1996).

2 An early treatment of the question of Italian-ness came from Giulio Bollati, significantly not a professional historian, in L'italiano: Il carattere nazionale come storia e come invenzione (Turin: Einaudi [1983] 1996). Recently the question of Italian national identity has become a veritable fixation with historians, spurred by the secessionist threats and dangers of disintegration. See G.E. Rusconi, Se cessiamo di essere una nazione (Bologna: Il Mulino, 1993); Aurelio Lepre, Italia addio? Unità e disunità dal 1860 a oggi (Milan: Mondadori, 1994); Ernesto Galli della Loggia, La morte della patria (Bari: Laterza, 1996); Beverly Allen and Mary Russo, eds., Revisioning Italy: National Identity and Global Culture (Minneapolis: University of Minnesota Press, 1997); Aldo Schiavone, Italiani senza Italia: Storia e identità (Turin: Einaudi, 1998); Albert R. Ascoli and Krystyna von Henneberg, eds., Making and Remaking Italy: The Cultivation of National Identity around the Risorgimento (Oxford and New York: Berg, 2001); Adrian Lyttelton, 'Creating a National Past: History, Myth and Image in the Risorgimento' in Making and Remaking, 27–74; and Silvana Patriarca, 'National Identity or National Character? New Vocabularies and Old Paradigms' in Making and Remaking, 299–319.

3 These are the years between the unification in 1861 and the official birthday of the Questione in 1876, when the Left came to power with the votes of the South. See Pasquale Villari, Le lettere meridionali ed altri scritti sulla questione sociale in Italia (Florence, [1875] 1878); Leopoldo Franchetti and Sidney Sonnino, Condizioni economiche ed amministrative delle province napoletane (Rome: Meridiana, 1992 (1875)); and La Sicilia nel 1876 (Florence:

Vallecchi, 1877). The growth of the *Questione* is a story of chain reactions, where legislative and state action interacts with public opinion in an imaginative complicity.

4 See Jane Schneider's 'Introduction' and essays by different authors in *Italy's Southern Question*; John Dickie, *Darkest Italy: The Nation and Stereotypes of the Mezzogiorno, 1860–1900* (New York: St Martin's Press, 1999); Nelson Moe, *The View from the Vesuvius* (Berkeley: University of California Press, 2002); Roberto Martucci, *L'invenzione dell'Italia unita: 1855–1864* (Milan: Sansoni, 1999); and Loredana Sciolla, *Italiani: Stereotipi di casa nostra* (Bologna: Il Mulino, 1997).

5 See Marta Petrusewicz, *Come il Meridione divenne Questione: Rappresentazioni del Sud prima e dopo il Quarantotto* (Soveria Mannelli: Rubbettino Editore, 1998).

6 Eric J. Hobsbawm, *Nations and Nationalisms since 1780* (Cambridge: Cambridge University Press, 1990). Significantly, Enrica Di Ciommo titles her book on the 1848 revolution in the Mezzogiorno *La nazione possibile: Mezzogiorno e questione nazionale nel 1848* (Milan: Franco Angeli, 1993), though it remains ambiguous as to which was the 'possible' nation in play – the Italian or the Neapolitan one.

7 The discussion of the 'ingredients' refers to the recent literature that has already become classical – for example, Anthony D. Smith, *The Ethnic Origins of Nations* (Oxford: Blackwell, 1986); Ernest Gellner, *Nations and Nationalism* (Oxford: Blackwell, 1983); Benedict Anderson, *Imagined Communities: Reflections on the Origin and Spread of Nationalism* (London: Verso-NLB, 1983).

8 In a perspicacious essay, Enrica Di Ciommo shows how the civil idea of national identity evolved, from the writings of Paolo Maria Doria at the beginning of the eighteenth century to the *Descrizione* by Giuseppe Maria Galanti at its end. See 'L'identità nazionale ed il Sud nel XVIII secolo' in *L'identità fra tradizione e progetto: nazioni, luoghi, culture* (Trento: Assessorato alla Cultura, 1996).

9 'Discorso preliminare' in Niccolo Caravita, *Niun diritto compete al sommo pontefice sul Regno di Napoli* (Aletopoli: [s.n.] 1790), xii.

10 Benedetto Croce, *Storia del Regno di Napoli* (Bari: Laterza, 1925), 174–5.

11 The subtle term is that of Vincenzo Cuoco ('La nostra nazione passava, per cosi dire, dalla fanciullezza alla sua gioventù'), who considered this a particularly vulnerable stage in the making of a national elite. *Saggio storico sulla rivoluzione napoletana del 1799* (Bari: Laterza, [1800] 1913), 64.

12 As he put it in a letter to his uncle Louis Philippe: 'Coll'aiuto di Dio, io

darò al mio popolo la prosperità e l'amministrazione onesta cui a' diritto, ma saró re *solo* e *sempre*.' Quoted in Di Ciommo, *La nazione possibile*, 21.

13 Francesco De Sanctis, *La giovinezza; memorie postume seguite da testimonianze biografiche di amici e discepoli*, ed. Gennaro Savarese (Turin: Einaudi, [1888] 1961), 293.

14 Pasquale Villari, *La giovinezza di Francesco de Sanctis, frammento autobiografico* (Naples: A. Morano, [1888] 1919), 336.

15 *Ristretto della storia della letteratura italiana* (Naples: Marotta e Vanspandock, 1883), 369.

16 *La nazione possibile*, 298–99.

17 Francesco Mastriani, *I Vermi: le classi pericolose in Napoli* (Naples: Luca Torre, [1863] 1994), 164.

18 Marion Miller, 'The Italian Revolutions and Regional Popular Culture' (unpublished paper, 1984).

19 Quoted in G. Zenobi, *Il triumviro Aurelio Saliceti* (Teramo: Ed. La Poligrafica, 1959), 92.

20 The article 'L'Italia e Murat' was published in Turin's *Diritto* on 5 October 1855 (year II, n. 236), and was one of De Sanctis's interventions in the 1855 debate around Murat's candidacy to the throne of Naples, to which I shall return below.

21 'Il Signore Gladstone ed il governo napoletano. Raccolta di scritti attorno alla questione napoletana' in W. Gladstone, *Lettere al Lord Aberdeen* (Turin: Tip. Ferrero e Franco, 1851), 11.

22 Giuseppe Ricciardi, 'preface' to the French edition of Luigi Settembrini *Protesta del popolo delle Due Sicilie*, in Franco Della Peruta, ed., *Scrittori politici dell'Ottocento* (Naples: Stampa, 1969), vol. I.

23 *Lettere dall'ergastolo*, ed. and with introduction by Mario Themelly (Milan: Feltrinelli, [1852] 1962), 81.

24 Letter to Giulio, April 1851, in Paolo Alatri, 'Lettere inedite di Antonio Scialoja,' *Movimento Operaio*, nn. 1–3, January–June 1956, part I: 161.

25 Anonymous [Francesco Trinchera di Ostumi], *La Quistione Napolitana: Ferdinando Borbone e Luciano Murat* (Italia, 1855), 26 ss.

26 Ibid.

Are We Dreaming? Exceptional Myths and Myths of Exceptionalism in the United States

FRANK UNGER

The playwright Arthur Miller recounts in his memoirs a story from an extended stay in Pyramid Lake, Nevada, during the mid-1950s. While establishing the six-week state residency required to obtain a divorce, he met two rodeo men who, between appearances, caught wild mustangs in the area. During their free time the two read westerns and dreamed of going to Hollywood to play cowboys on the silver screen. Miller drew from this acquaintance while writing the screenplay for the film *The Misfits*. Back in Nevada four years later with the crew that was shooting the film, Miller, since married to the film's female star, Marilyn Monroe, met the two rodeo men again. The old friendship was soon strained when the two became obtrusive and obsequious, constantly asking about western film stars and urging their new friend, who undoubtedly had Hollywood connections, to help them obtain a Hollywood contract to play cowboys.

'My two friends couldn't understand,' wrote Miller, 'why I thought it strange that men who had lived on horseback for years looked to the movies for their models and could imagine no finer fate than to be picked up for a film role. The movie cowboy was the real one, they the imitations.'[1]

This story could be used to introduce various discussions and reflections on American culture and society: the difficulty of human connections in a commercialized world; the American dream of being 'famous' and the importance of so-called 'celebrities'; or, superficially, the importance of the silver screen for the world view of many Americans. Former President Ronald Reagan, for example, often recounted at press conferences scenes from feature films as 'examples from history.' But I would like to use this story to introduce a more general theme: the subordinate role of reality in American culture, or, respectively, the nearly total predominance of imagination over fact in what Americans generally 'know' about their own country, and the effects of this, not only on the country's own society and politics, but also on outsiders' perceptions of and beliefs about the United States. It is true that every nation-state is an 'imagined community' whose citizens generally share some mythical beliefs about an alleged common past reaching back to times when the nation did not yet exist. The United States, however, does not have an ancient past. Its myths therefore must draw on more recent events, nearly all of them very well documented. Those myths can therefore be, and have been, disproved by scholars many times, but that is of no importance. More than any other country in the world, the United States demonstrates the function and persistence of national myths and their immunity from critics who would introduce un-glamorous concepts such as historical accuracy.

I

The ruling elites of post-feudal societies had to ensure the cohesion and deference of the lower classes without the supporting legitimacy of traditional hierarchies. There was no longer a sacred order or divine law of kings to keep everyone in their ancestral place, nor did identification with the glory of heavenly authority compensate for the misery and injustices of the common people's everyday life. This was especially true for the United States of America after its declaration of political and economic independence in 1776, for this act cut off American civil society from its former symbolic source of legitimacy, the British Crown.

Nearly all modern historians extol the momentous character of the 'American Revolution.' The German historian Udo Sautter, for example, writes in his *History of the United States* (1976): 'Certainly the American rebellion was the struggle of a colonized people for their independence, and therefore, if one will, the great archetype for similar movements during the next two centuries. However, it was at the same time the revolt of a subject people against a hereditary crown, and thus a role model for all domestic revolutions from 1789 to the present.'[2]

Sautter's take on the founding of the United States (in essence the same interpretation as that given by countless other authors, including American Marxists) is far from being the honest conclusion of diligent research. It has nothing to do with research or scholarship at all. It is only the due citation of the myth on which the United States is founded, and since the book is written for educated readers, the author is simply touching base with that myth. For this conception of the United States' 'revolutionary' democratic origins – that it was born from a metaphysical faith in reason and egalitarianism coupled with a desire to realize human rights, all made legitimate through the *Declaration of Independence*, which proclaimed even the *pursuit of happiness* to be an *unalienable right* – is deeply embossed on the collective consciousness of the modern West, and beyond. It is, as it were, a worldwide political trademark. Its articulation, whether incidental or emphatic, simply signals that the author wishes to align himself with the dominant discourse community.

It does not matter that, as any careful consideration of the available documents and sources reveals, this reading of the origin of the United States is at most a half-truth. The leaders of the North American rebellion against the British Crown in 1776 did not represent an oppressed colonial people, nor were they themselves actually oppressed. And their thoughts on the political organization of the newly independent thirteen colonies were not original, nor did they claim to be the result of deep thinking, let alone any kind of utopian vision. As Morton White has noted, 'they wrote their philosophy as they ran.'[3] And how could they have done otherwise? Rather than hoping to put theoretical ideals into practice, they were fully occupied with legitimizing their actions to the outside world. In short, besides being the founding fathers of the country, they were also its first masters of spin.

The task of the founding fathers was to drum up popular support for secession from Britain without provoking populist sedition at home. They were in the delicate situation of having to justify rebellion against established monarchical authority without, at the same time, prompting a more general questioning of authority, especially their own. Accordingly, they were very circumspect; in no way did they call upon their countrymen to 'Sapere aude!' (Have courage to use your own reason!). Around that time, with those words, in *The Philosophy of Reason*, German philosopher Immanuel Kant was challenging his sleepy fellow Germans to follow the self-evident truths that could be found through the rigorous application of one's innate reason.[4] In contrast, the American founding fathers' concept of 'self-evident truth,' drawn from John Locke's theory of knowledge, remained firmly within the tradition of natural law. Ever since Aquinas, natural law had held that not everyone possessed rationality; consequently, not everyone had access to 'self-evident truth.' Certain prerequisites were needed – such as 'education' and 'property.'

This was not the only occasion that the founding fathers stayed safely on the conservative side of the contemporary European discourse on natural law: the so-called American belief in the pursuit of happiness reflects a phrase that was common currency in eighteenth-century European discourse. It was specifically rooted in the work of Jean Jacques Burlamaqui (1694–1748), a Swiss-Italian lawyer who, among the many popularizers of Lockeian ideas for the continental propertied classes, was favoured by many of the founding fathers, in particular James Wilson and Thomas Jefferson. Burlamaqui was seen as an authoritative contemporary on political issues and was often cited in their debates on natural law.[5]

The point here is not to deflate the myth that the American founding fathers were independent and original political thinkers. But that myth still deserves to be analysed in its contemporary political context. And given the political discourse current among European intellectuals at the time of the Declaration of Independence, it is useful to note which ideas appealed to the American elite; which political models they thought would add legitimacy to their revolt (in Europe) and to their continued leadership (at home); and which ones they avoided mentioning. For Locke and Burlamaqui were certainly not the only eighteenth-century European political theorists drawing from the tenets of natural law. For example, Jean-Jacques Rousseau, not only today but then as well, was better known than Burlamaqui. Moreover, one would think that his concept of the 'social contract' would be ideally suited for legitimizing a newly established democratic commonwealth of free and equal citizens. Like Locke, Rousseau's ideas were based on the premise that 'in nature,' people were free, equal, and inherently good. However, Rousseau did not strike a chord with the American founding fathers. After all, he maintained that it was the establishment of private property which brought to human society the problem of inequality and consequently corruption and violence. For Rousseau, slavery was anathema. For Locke however, social inequality – including black slavery – was not a problem but rather the justifiable result of natural differences between individuals' preferences, talents, and 'possession of rational power.'

This was also the line of thinking followed by the leaders of the American War for Independence. It was certainly not the world view of a colonized people striving for freedom. It was the perspective of an expatriate English gentry, striving for freedom from infringements on what they considered their own business, in the literal sense of the word. For good reason, John Locke was their philosopher of choice. What appealed to them about Locke was his genial ambiguity, which on the one hand allowed them to legitimize their disobedience to the British monarch, and on the other hand allowed them to defend the domestic social order in the liberated colonies against challenges 'from below' – that is, from those who didn't own property or were not of English descent and, thus, *in* but not *of* civil society. For Locke, for all practical purposes, only property owners were essentially *rational* human beings. For this reason he assigned faith a legitimate place next to reason. Once the English gentry had realigned the hegemonic structures in their society to accommodate their interests, using natural rights arguments, for obvious reasons they wanted to forestall the non-propertied classes from legitimizing upsetting social demands on their behalf by likewise appealing to reason and natural rights. Consequently, rationality was assigned to the preserve of the 'educated' classes, whereas religion could henceforth continue to comfort the working poor; any insubordination on the latter's part could duly be attributed to 'irrationality.'

The American founding fathers were very much at home with this kind of paternalistic 'dualism.' The North American colonies already had two hundred years of history under their belt, and the leaders calling for independence were no *sans-culottes*, but representatives of the colonies' political and economic elite. With their Constitution of 1788–9, they created a political system based firmly on the ideology of 'possessive individualism' and designed to secure the hegemony of the new American gentry. It was explicitly intended to contain the dangers of democracy: elected representatives, not the people themselves, were to rule. Obliged to their convictions, independent from any specific mandates of their constituents, these representatives were to be a unified body of 'trustees' administering the Commonwealth.[6] What a wonderful Romantic idea – the establishment of a governing elite interested only in promoting the common good, free from all economic and political special interests, elected to their offices not for their promised determination to carry through sectarian programs, but solely because of their individual integrity and incorruptibility. A wonderful idea, yes, but not democratic.

One could ask, so what? At issue is the establishment of a political union back in the eighteenth century. How can one expect to find democracy in the modern sense? Haven't the social and democratic failings of the original Constitution been amended over the past two centuries? The obvious answer – 'yes' – is not as self-evident as it may seem. Undoubtedly the constitutional realities of the United States have evolved since it was established. No one can deny that it has been moving toward our modern understanding of 'democracy' – in terms of both a broader foundation and a greater social consciousness. But has constitutional change been great enough to eliminate the bias toward oligarchy and propertied-class autocracy that was built in by the founding fathers? At the beginning of the twenty-first century, are the societal foundations and social elements of 'American democracy' still up to acceptable global standards?

II

Since the pitiful collapse of the only 'really existing' historical alternative to capitalism, questions like these seem – at first sight – even more out of touch with reality than before. The sacrosanct status that America and its 'free-market system' now enjoy among elites in most parts of the world drowns out attention to questions such as these. Even in the discourses of European intellectuals, who have traditionally been more class-sensitive than their American counterparts, people who want to raise concerns about social equality, social justice, or social anything are nowadays likely to bemuse their peers. With this, one could argue, the Americanization of Europe, long lamented by conservatives, has reached a new high point. After all, nothing is more American than the rhetorical demonization of 'socialism.' Despite the widely held beliefs about 'pragmatic' and 'non-ideological' America, the spreading of negative connotations about anything 'social' has long been a hallmark of 'Americanism.' All true Americans have to pay it lip service, or suffer – not in the courts, but through community reprisals and political isolation.

Experts on ideology from all political camps vigorously dispute the often-heard argument that Americans are antisocialist precisely because of their aversion to ideologies as such, and are therefore by definition 'pragmatic' and non-ideological. For example, in 1935 a disappointed socialist, Leon Samson, wrote: 'Americanism isn't something which relates to a cultural tradition or a place, but is instead a doctrine – that which, for a socialist, socialism is.'[7] In his seminal book *An American Dilemma*, the liberal Swedish scholar Gunnar Myrdal wrote of an 'American creed.'[8] The conservative scholar Samuel P. Huntington used the same phrase in *American Politics: The Promise of Disharmony*.[9]

There is ample evidence that something like a 'mandatory' world view for American citizens existed long before the provocation of organized socialism, the foremost enemy of the United States since the Russian Revolution. Alexis de Tocqueville makes several allusions in this direction, and his contemporary, the Austrian Francis Grund, provides a concise summary of this phenomenon. In the 1830s Grund spent seven years living in and travelling across the United States. Grund wrote a series of insightful books about his experiences, and we can regret that he has been overshadowed by Tocqueville. In his most famous book he addresses the question of American patriotism and gives us the first prophetic depiction of Americanism as an expansionist belief system:

> An American does not love his country as a Frenchman loves France, or an Englishman England: America is to him but the physical means of establishing a moral power – the medium through which his mind operates – the 'local habitation' of his political doctrines. His country is in his understanding; he carries it with him wherever he goes, whether he emigrates to the shores of the Pacific or the Gulf of Mexico; his home is wherever he finds minds congenial with his own.
>
> Americans have been reproached with want of love for their own country; but, with such an enlightened attachment to their moral and political institutions, it is difficult to fix upon them the limits of the empire which must eventually be theirs, or upon the boundary line which they shall not overleap in their progress. The patriotism of the Americans is not confined either to a love of their country, or to those who are of the same origin with them: it is related to the mind, and to the habits of thinking and reasoning. Whoever thinks as they do, is, morally speaking, a citizen of their community; and whoever entertains opinions in opposition to their established theory of government, must be considered a natural enemy of their country.[10]

Huntington, for his part, defines the core content of the American Creed as 'Freedom, equality, individualism, democracy and the principle of constitutionally guaranteed legality.'[11] A more comprehensive definition might be possible if one drew together the popular images of two classical works: John Locke's above-mentioned *Two Treatises of Civil Government* and Adam Smith's *The Wealth of Nations*. In other words, the American Creed amalgamates the imaginations of a liberal republic of propertied citizens with the 'market driven' system of competitive production and distribution, within which – as described in the introductory chapter of *The Wealth of Nations* – producers provide for the greatest common good by independently pursuing their individual self-interest.

Even so, one should not confuse a creed with a legal code or a policy guideline, and at least in the case of Adam Smith, this interpretation does not provide for even a remotely accurate reading of the source. The most important aspect of a creed is the confession attached to it. A confession is a rhetorical act: both a sign connoting voluntary membership in a community, and a means of community solidarity. This solidarity can legitimate a community's censure of one of its members. Breaking a law or ignoring a policy results in a prescribed systematic sanction. Public blasphemy against a creed, however, inevitably requires excommunication. In the United States, since its founding, the utterly secular striving for individual gain has been cast in terms that approach a religious value. In other words, the rhetorical presentation of simple gain-oriented individualism as a quasi-earthly epitome of the Kingdom of Heaven – directly derived from the Puritan interpretation of the Old Testament – functions very much like a confession in a religious community.

Despite these rather uninspired objectives for their *covenant*, for Americans, *America* was and is more than just another place in the wilderness of this world. Its rhetoric declares it to be the 'New Canaan.' At a time when revolutions and class struggles were brewing almost everywhere in the Old World, challenging old and new authorities alike, Herman Melville wrote about the New World in his novel *White-jacket*:

> Escaped from the house of bondage, Israel of old did not follow after the ways of the Egyptians. To her was given an express dispensation; to her were given new things under the sun. And we Americans are the peculiar, chosen people – the Israel of our time; we bear the ark of the liberties of the world. Seventy years ago we escaped from thrall; and, besides our first birthright – embracing one continent of earth – God has given to us, for a future inheritance, the broad domains of the political pagans, that shall yet come and lie down under the shade of our ark, without bloody hands being lifted. God has predestinated, mankind expects great things from our race; and great things we feel in our souls. The rest of the nations must soon be in our rear. We are the pioneers of the world; the advance-guard, sent on through the wilderness of untried things, to break a new path in the New World that is ours. In our youth is our strength; in our inexperi-

ence, our wisdom. At a period when other nations have but lisped, our deep voice is heard afar. Long enough have we been skeptics with regard to ourselves, and doubted whether indeed, the political Messiah had come. But he has come in us, if we would but give utterance to his promptings. And let us always remember that with ourselves, almost for the first time in the history of earth, national selfishness is unbounded philanthropy; for we cannot do a good to America but we give alms to the world.[12]

One could reasonably surmise that, written at a time when 'young America' was still largely a socially homogeneous Arcadia of the free and independent yeomen farmers Thomas Jefferson saw as the foundation for political democracy, this vision of America as 'political Messiah' was an enthusiastic reflection of a still largely egalitarian social order. Only later would the hope of maintaining and refining this society of free and equal citizens prove futile. But this does not make sense. One should not overlook the fact that Melville was writing at a time when one out of five Americans was either a black slave or a Native American, and thus not even considered a citizen. Nor did anything resembling a state of equality exist among the white majority. Working with irrefutable statistics, practitioners of the New Economic History have already pulled the rug out from under the myth of Jacksonian Democracy. One out of eight white Americans was not an immigrant from England, and thus not worthy of the Ark of the Covenant. In the cities along the eastern seaboard, where one needed an annual income of around a thousand dollars to meet the English standard of being 'middle class,' only 1 per cent of the population earned more than eight hundred dollars a year. Moreover, since the time the new Children of Israel were freed from their Egyptian servitude, American society had become more economically and politically stratified. The Canadian scholar Sacvan Bercovitch remarks: 'When Samuel Danforth gave his famous sermon on New England's mission in the wilderness in 1670, the top five percent of the chosen ones owned a quarter of society's wealth. A hundred years later ... thus when independence was achieved from Great Britain, three percent of those eligible to vote owned a third of the national wealth. In 1849, when this vanguard declared itself the political Messiah, one percent of Americans owned almost half of the country's wealth.'[13]

Let us be clear about this: these figures are in no way historically exceptional. For example, the former British motherland had a very similar division of wealth and a comparable oligarchical political system. But only in the United States of America was the ruling property-owning class able to successfully cover this thoroughly conventional and undistinguished social situation with a rhetoric suggesting that this was a direct fulfilment of Biblical prophecy. And this at a time when the legal system permitted something that was explicitly denounced several times in the Bible: the ownership of other human beings! Bercovitch comments:

> For more than two centuries the symbol of 'America' promised immigrants that by crossing the ocean they could remove their old world garments, jump into the melting pot, and come out as complete Americans. And when, as was almost always the case, the experience did not live up to expectations, the immigrants found apparent compensation in the rhetoric itself. Discrimination, poverty, alienation – symbolically understood, weren't these simply transitional tests like those encountered by the children of Israel on their way to the new Jerusalem?[14]

The key words here are 'compensation in the rhetoric itself.' How else does one explain how only one generation after Melville's sentimental statement, the United States was practically the only modern industrial state to go through the process of capitalist industrialization without producing a sustainable *national* party representing the working classes and devoted to the political aim of overcoming or seriously reforming capitalism – especially when one considers that the American wheels of progress often outdid their European equivalents in brutality and required human grease? As the German economic historian Werner Sombart asked in bewilderment at precisely this point in history: 'Why is there no socialism in the United States?'[15]

III

Variants of the frontier thesis have often been offered as an answer. Developed by the American historian Frederick Jackson Turner in the 1890s, this thesis maintains that the so-called *frontier* – the decades-long existence of open, unsettled land in the West – was the deciding factor in the creation of an autochthonous American society and political culture.[16] The possibility of open expansion and escape within the nation's own borders served as a 'safety valve,' one that permitted industrialization with all its ruthless disciplinarianism while ensuring that the ruling classes need not concern themselves about political stability. Immigrant wage slaves and native middle-class losers could imagine their fate as only temporary, as long as the possibility of autonomy and a 'new beginning' theoretically existed out West. This mitigated against feelings of despair over one's individual fate and over lost battles for a stake in the Gilded Age society – both important elements for the development of collectivist ideologies.[17]

The frontier thesis has some validity; however, it does not entirely explain why no organized working-class-based political movement – be it moderate social-democratic or radical communist – was ever able to gain a lasting foothold in American political culture. Other areas of Anglo-Saxon expansion, namely Australia and Canada, had a similar frontier situation as the United States, yet in those countries socialist or social democratic ideas and movements have never taken on an analogous stigma of being 'un-Australian' or 'un-Canadian.' So why, then, in the United States? The only explanation is that the propertied classes in the United States succeeded in buttressing the capitalist economic system with the emotional and rhetorical sinews of religious conviction and utopian sanguinity: a stabilizing sleight of hand beyond the dreams of the European propertied classes.

From time to time, concern was voiced that the American Dream of individualistically pursued happiness was futile, possibly even a deception promoted to support the system. On such occasions, efforts were then made to organize a movement based on this political premise, rather than around an ethnic group or religious conviction. Yet in such cases, it was rarely the state that came forward to check these potentially unruly individuals and their radical ideas. Mainstream culture, as strong as any dictator, quickly denounced them as 'un-American,' effectively silencing their dissent or neutralizing it by forcing them to articulate radical ideas in terms acceptable to American rhetoric. During the 1930s, American communists tried to declare Lenin the Thomas Jefferson of the twentieth century. The slogan 'Communism is the Americanism of the twentieth century' was used to promote the Popular Front. During the 1960s, with few exceptions, students and others protesting the Vietnam War called on the United States to return to its historical role as the world's political saviour and ethical role model.[18]

It would be wrong to see only oratorical opportunism when radical movements make such all-American appeals. It is possible that there were individual cases when Americanism was intentionally used to candy-coat radical propaganda, but these were certainly rare exceptions. It is more likely that, in most cases, even political radicals took such sentiments deeply to heart. Bercovitch implies this: 'The United States is a country, perhaps the only in the world, whose spiritual base is found in its rhetoric.'[19] It is the foundation on which all must stand who want to play an active role in national political life. Long before someone even begins to consciously consider his or her political goals, the rhetoric of the polity has already established a constraint that shapes one's perceptions of reality, and the very categories with which one thinks and conceives meaning. In other words, the rhetoric of Americanism plays a significant role in creating good American citizens. It is especially well internalized by those who take part in political life for unselfish reasons.

Let us return again to the earlier quotation from Herman Melville's *White-jacket* and that amazing sentence: 'National selfishness is unbounded philanthropy; for we cannot do a good to America but we give alms to the world.' Bercovitch had this to say about it:

What is meaningful about this platitude is its ideological arrogance. Patriotism is one thing, but to identify the interest of a nation – and furthermore one which has elevated selfishness to its highest dogma – with the welfare of humankind is clearly something else: namely chauvinism in the service of free enterprise ... The loyalist Protestants may have introduced work ethics to Canada, but the Puritans of New England have bequeathed the myth of America to capitalism.[20]

Later in his life Melville became bitter after losing his faith in America as the political Messiah. But like many other intellectuals who followed him in taking issue with their country and culture – shifting from the extremes of deification to damnation – he never succeeded in escaping the myth of America, and thus he was never able to soberly judge the United States' strengths and weaknesses. The American myth still has an effect on its critics and on the enemies of its politics and culture – this is perhaps the most remarkable observation one can make about this nation. Thus, even those who wish to 'deconstruct' the United States' claims of exceptionalism, and who explicitly make it their task to examine that nation as simply another country, must acknowledge this fact, whether they like it or not: the United States is exceptional in this world. It is exceptional because of the existence and power of the concept of *America*. Nowhere else, with so little public coercion and police control, is there such willingness to live within such a strict and narrow system of cultural norms. Nowhere else is it a foregone conclusion that all societal conflict will be addressed within a compulsory rhetoric of political orthodoxy that leaves the majority of those in society not only effectively numb against arguments critical of the system, but highly receptive to any political manipulation in support of the status quo.

IV

In a 1967 empirical study, Lloyd Free and Hadly Cantril discovered that the political convictions of Americans have two dimensions: one 'operational,' the other 'ideological.' They observed that popular opinion about any given topic could be totally contradictory, depending on how the question was framed. For example, the vast majority of those surveyed were for the 'introduction of a socially organized, comprehensive medical care system for all American citizens.' However, by about the same majority, the same proposal was clearly rejected when the question mentioned 'socialized medicine.' From this, Free and Cantril concluded that the 'operational' dimension of American political consciousness was social-democratic and egalitarian, whereas the 'ideological' side was conservative.[21]

What is most interesting about this dualism is not that it exists, but that whenever there is conflict between the operational and the ideological dimensions of American political consciousness, as a rule the ideological wins. Bluntly stated, the rhetoric of individualistic Americanism can be called out to manipulate the majority of Americans to be against their own objective social interests. This is why, for the past half-century, the American Medical Association and other special interest groups have been able to block the introduction of a comprehensive national health care system.

Nonetheless, what seems to be an incomprehensible denial of obvious self-interest in favour of ideological principles by a majority does have a covert socio-psychological plausibility. This socio-psychological plausibility is revealed in the American nation's unspoken, well-known, but deeply closeted family secret – namely, the political, social, and emotional relationship between the white American majority and the 20-some per cent of their fellow citizens who have African ancestry. Today the potential explosive force of the so-called race problem is no longer vividly demonstrated in ghetto riots and civil rights marches, but rather in everyday news reports. For example, on 31 March 1987 the *Detroit Free Press* mentioned that the mayor of Detroit, Coleman Young, had made a statement on youth criminality in his city. At a press conference the mayor's office released a new statistical report on the city's crime rates for 1986. According to this report, 365 children under seventeen had been injured by gunfire in the inner city of Detroit in 1986. Forty-three of these gunshot wounds had been fatal; the youngest victim was four years old. All of these victims were African American. The rate for the current year was not quite as bad, but still troubling. The Detroit newspaper's accompanying sense of concern was as if the news had been filed from some country far removed, rather than from its own city.

The reason a civilized society like the United States could react to such bad news in its midst with such incomprehensible indifference is that those immediately affected were black. That is, they were the direct descendants of those African tribes whom the world's new political Messiah had been dragging for almost another century to their country to work as slaves in their capitalist plantation economy. These former slaves have long since developed their own genuine American culture, yet the white majority still today maintains that form of hate-filled distance that all historical culprits (especially some Christian denominations) bear toward their victims. This animosity cannot be overcome with reason because it is derived from a secret collective fear of God's wrath – in this case, historical retribution. Truly granting American blacks affirmative action, social status, and equality would be the equivalent of confessing to a historical crime – one that white Americans committed during the time of their supposed great democratic blossoming. In order to maintain a distance from this phenotypic Other in their own backyard (while also maintaining the derived sense of societal privilege), most poor white Americans still today renounce all class-specific demands on their societal superiors and refuse to see through the rhetoric of individualism and self-sufficiency, as long as this allows them to eclipse the poor blacks in the unspoken hierarchy of the land.[22]

Despite all the advances that have been made in civil rights over the last forty years – largely related to the acceptance of a white-cultivated black elite – the continued effective racism of American society is not merely a moral or socio-political problem. It affects more than just African Americans themselves and those whites who are nearest them on the social ladder. The affluent suburbanite also pays a price if, because of the terrible rate of violent death among teenagers, the life expectancy for a newborn African American in Harlem is only nineteen years. Most members of the former slave-owning race fearfully avoid setting foot in certain sections of the large cities. White residents of Washington, Boston, Chicago, Cleveland, Philadelphia, and Detroit must constantly visualize an alternative map of the city demarcating where it is safe for them to go and which streets, bridges, and intersections they should avoid crossing, although in many cases the dangers said to await them may well not exist. Fear and projected expectations of violence create paths of their own. The university town of London, Ontario, barely 180 kilometres from the Michigan border, every week-end experiences an invasion by thousands of well-off Greater Detroit residents. They come primarily for one reason – to enjoy the luxury of being able to go out in a genuine city environment for dinner in a quaint and friendly restaurant, and then to be able to go for a short after-dinner stroll, or bar-hopping, without fear of witnessing or becoming innocent victims of a gunfight.

It has often been said that the proverbial American Dream has become a nightmare. This is true and false at the same time. First, 'America' in its long history has never been what millions of people throughout the world thought it to be, and in some ways still do. A life of freedom, prosperity, and independence has always been in the United States, as in all known societies of the world, the privilege of a minority. The masses of 'little people' from Europe, who were supposedly drawn by the American Dream across the Atlantic during the last third of the nineteenth century, were in part rural poor who would have gone anywhere for the promise of work. Others were simply victims of demographic pressures and migration-driven processes. About one-third of them returned to the Old World after a few years.[23] For the great majority of American citizens, black and white, life consisted of intermittent work, degradation, and a struggle to survive. Unlike in other parts of the world, their scourge wasn't oppression by the police and regimentation by the state. That was not necessary, because they received both directly from private employers, who exercised in many parts of the country quasi-official authority that differed from state authority only in that there was no legal method of appeal. In this way, individual rights could be circumvented despite the rhetoric of protection found in the American Bill of Rights. The majority of the people in the United States were much too busy trying to make a living to dream the American Dream.

It was only with the Second World War and the resulting changes in the employment structure and the economic role of the government that the United States was first able to create something like general prosperity for more than a small minority of its citizens. For the masses of white Americans, this prosperity brought an abundance of food, cheaply manufactured mass products, and the privilege of owning one's own home, complete with electrical appliances and a car or two. This was the American Dream of the 1950s and 1960s. It was dreamed of above all in Europe, where the war's destruction made such symbols of the good life remain luxuries for a few years longer.

Today, most of western Europe and many other countries throughout the world have caught up with the United States in terms of consumption and cheap, mass-produced consumer goods. Western Europeans' former adulation and admiration for America is being replaced by a growing sense of aggravation and annoyance over the perceived smugness, self-righteous arrogance, and non-cooperative solipcism of the hegemonic American culture.

V

One of former President Clinton's favourite aphorisms was that 'there is nothing wrong with America that can't be cured by what's right with America.' What the president was actually evoking with this sentiment was no more and no less than a claim that the United States remains the only country in the world that simply has nothing to learn from anyone abroad. All answers must come from within.

The problem the rest of the world increasingly sees with this kind of imperturbable solipsism is that it is now shared by more Americans than ever before. It seems to have captured even the country's most critical and cosmopolitan intellectuals. They may occasionally quote Benjamin, Nietzsche, or Sartre in their scholarly works, but they regularly refer to the Declaration of Independence and the Constitution (and mix them up sometimes) whenever they address questions of democracy and politics in their own country. A non-American's humble question – Why do they go along with the custom of glorifying a constitution drafted at the end of the eighteenth century by a closely-knit group of self-interested merchants and slaveholders? – would be regarded not only as extremely rude, but also as utterly ignorant. For don't we all know that Americans may mess up a lot of things at home or in other parts of the world, but they always do it with good intentions? They always try to give 'a more perfect meaning to the thing we started with – the Constitution and the Bill of Rights.'[24] So whatever they do, they always wind up 'more perfect' than when they started.

NOTES

1 Arthur Miller, *Timebends: A Life* (New York: Grove Press, 1987), 382.
2 Udo Sautter, *Geschichte der Vereinigten Staaten von Amerika* (Stuttgart: Kröner, 1976), 65.
3 Morton White, *The Philosophy of the American Revolution* (New York: Oxford University Press, 1978), 4.
4 Immanuel Kant, 'What Is Enlightenment' (1784) in *On []History: Immanuel Kant*, edited by Lewis White Beck (Indianapolis: Bobbs-Merrill Company, 1963), 3.
5 White, *Philosophy*, 36 ff.
6 See William A. Williams, 'Amerika — Die ermattete und nostalgische Kultur,' in *Amerikanische Mythen*, edited by Frank Unger (Frankfurt/M.: Campus, 1988), 267 ff.
7 Leon Samson, *Toward a United Front* (New York: Farrar & Rinehart, Inc., 1935), 16.
8 Gunnar Myrdal, *An American Dilemma* (New York: McGraw-Hill, 1964), I:4.
9 Samuel P. Huntington, *American Politics: The Promise of Disharmony* (Cambridge, MA: Belknap Press, 1981), 23 ff.
10 Francis J. Grund, *The Americans in Their Moral, Social and Political Relations* (Boston: Marsh, Caper, & Lyon, 1837/Reprint New York and London: Longman, 1968), 149.
11 Huntington, *American Politics*, 24.
12 Herman Melville, *White-jacket* (London: Collins, original 1850), 184–5 (ch. 36).
13 Sacvan Bercovitch, 'Konsens und Anarchie: Die Funktion der Rhetorik für die amerikanische Identität,' in *Amerikanische Mythen*, 25.
14 Ibid., 27.
15 Werner Sombart, *Warum gibt es in den Vereinigten Staaten keinen Sozialismus?* (Tübingen: J.C.B. Mohr, 1906), republished in *Archiv für Sozialwissenschaft und Sozialpolitik*, Band 21.
16 Frederick Jackson Turner, *The Significance of the Frontier in American History* (Ann Arbor: University microfilms, 1966), reprint from the *Annual Report of the American Historical Association* (1893).

17 See Henry Nash Smith, *Virgin Land: The American West as Symbol and Myth* (Cambridge: Harvard University Press, 1970), 201 ff.
18 See Todd Gitlin, *The Sixties: Years of Hope, Days of Rage* (New York and Toronto: Bantam, 1987), especially 187 ff.
19 Bercovitch, 'Konsens und Anarchie,' 30.
20 Ibid., 31–2.
21 Lloyd Free and Hadley Cantril, *The Political Beliefs of Americans* (New Brunswick: NJ: Rutgers University Press, 1967).
22 See Remco van Capelleveen's, 'Rassismus und "American Dream": Zur Lebenswirklichkeit der afro-amerikanischen Bevölkerung in den USA,' and 'Middle Class Society Made in USA – oder Der amerikanische "Abschied vom Proletariat"' both in Unger, *Amerikanische Mythen,* 81–112 and 233–66.
23 See Robert Burchell, 'Die Einwanderung nach Amerika im 19. und 20. Jahrhundert,' in *Die Vereinigten Staaten von Amerika, Fischer Weltgeschichte Bd. 30,* edited by Willi Paul Adams (Franfurt am Main: Fischer, 1977), 184–234, especially 208 ff; as well as Ekkehart Krippendorff, 1978, 'Migrationsbewegungen und die Herausbildung des kapitalistischen Weltmarkts,' in *Die Dritte Welt* 6(1), 74–106.
24 White House Press Release, *Discussion Remarks (by President Clinton) in Town Hall Meeting on One America,* 3 December 1997.

The Republic: A French Myth

Among the political myths that shape the French collective mind, the myth of the Republic is probably the most influential and certainly the most controversial. It is a very particular idea of the Republic, which used to be undisputed and has now been called into question. Yet it remains at the centre of French political debate.

The French historian Raoul Girardet wrote a book fifteen years ago about French political myths and mythologies. He studied four of them that he thought typical of French politics: the myth of conspiracy, the myth of the saviour (from Napoleon to de Gaulle), the myth of the Golden Age, and the myth of unity. The myth of the Republic is closely connected to this last myth, the myth of unity.[1]

The way most columnists and politicians in France reacted to the last American presidential election is quite indicative of the French view of the Republic. They talked about this election – as you may guess – in a very scornful manner. They said that what happened in Florida was clear evidence of a crisis in the American style of democracy as opposed to that of the French Republic.

Why were we so bewildered by the outcome of the election? Why – apart from our old anti-Americanism – were we so critical of the electoral process in the United States? Why did we believe this election was not really a democratic one?

The answer: because of our idea of the Republic, which is exactly the opposite of the American idea, at least as we see it. I would like to focus on three main differences between the French and American systems – three main reasons for being amazed, when you are French, by the American democratic process:

- The federal system, which gives a lot of power to the states but is at odds with our own view of democracy. We cannot understand how a candidate can be elected when he has got fewer votes than his opponent, even if we know it is because of the federal system.
- The relationship between justice and politics, in particular the crucial role given to the Supreme Court. We cannot understand how judges can decide who will be the next president, nor can we acknowledge the idea of the Supreme Court deciding the outcome of an election.
- The selection of American politicians, the way they emerge and reach important positions. We cannot understand how a great country like the United States can elect a president who is widely regarded as provincial, much as Jimmy Carter, Ronald Reagan, and even Bill Clinton were regarded in the past elections. We think our presidents must be the best and the brightest, graduates of our *grandes écoles* and part of the Paris elite. This is closely connected, I think, to our faith in our school system.

The republican myth in France is based on the rejection of the three principles that constitute the pillars of the American Republic: federalism, that is to say the primacy of the member states over the nation; the rule of law, that is to say the primacy of judges over politicians; and the belief that anybody can become president of the United States, even if he or she was not a brilliant and accomplished student.

In contrast, our Republic – as it is understood by many French people – has three pillars: centralization, which means that France is and must remain a single, unitary, and indivisible republic; the will of the people, which means that the law, as it is passed by the Parliament, must prevail over the will of the judges; and the school system, which is the driving force of so-called republican elitism.

These three topics have been, and continue to be, the source of many controversies in France. They derive from the above-mentioned idea of the Republic, which is advocated by many people in intellectual and political circles.

The controversy surrounding the first topic – the unity of the Republic – was revived recently when the question of the future of Corsica was raised by the government. Prime Minister Lionel Jospin promised to grant some sort of autonomy to the island. The so-called republicans replied that if the provinces were granted political powers, French identity might be jeopardized and the country might become a pure aggregation of territories without a strong unity.

In regard to the second topic – a government of judges as a substitute for the legitimate republican government – the debate dealt with the powers of the Constitutional Council (the French Supreme Court), which had recently cancelled some important parliamentary decisions and was being accused of encroaching on the powers of politicians.

The third topic is connected to the longstanding debate about the French school system, which led to the removal of the Minister of Education last year, after huge demonstrations by teachers.

Corsica

The island of Corsica is one of the French provinces that harbours regionalist, autonomist, even nationalist claims. Such claims also exist in the Basque country, but they are much stronger on the Spanish side of the border than on the French side. In Brittany, Alsace, and even Savoy, where such claims can be found as well, they are supported only by a small minority of people. In Corsica, where for at least the past twenty-five years there has been an armed conflict linked to dozens of killings – including the murder of Claude Erignac, the government envoy, in 1998 – the nationalist movement has real electoral power (about 25 per cent of the vote in regional elections). A majority of members in the Corsican assembly, whether nationalists or not, support institutional changes that would grant Corsicans greater autonomy.

These changes are currently under discussion, and they are deeply upsetting to Jacobin republicans. One of the most controversial issues is the teaching of the Corsican language, which would be included in the curriculum of all students unless their parents forbid it. Another concerns the right of the Corsican assembly to adapt some of the laws passed by the French national assembly, which would give Corsican representatives some part of the legislative power. This power, according to republican principles, should belong exclusively to members of the national Parliament in the name of the people's sovereignty.

To grant regional representatives the right to participate in the making of laws, even under very particular conditions, means – to those who oppose such a move in the name of the Republic – endangering the unity of the Republic by heading toward federalism. This, they claim, is at odds with French history, since 1789 and even before. As President Chirac put it in a televised speech, if this happens, either Corsica will part from the French Republic or France will stop being a 'unitary Republic' and become a 'federation of regions.'

A similar debate took place a few years ago over the concept of a 'Corsican people.' It was in 1990, when a projected reform for Corsica mentioned 'the Corsican people, [as a] component of the French people.' Over strong protests from some socialists – in particular Jean-Pierre Chevènement, then Minister of Defence and one of the most prominent Jacobin republicans – these words were voted in by the National Assembly. They were afterwards rejected by the Constitutional Council. Why? Because the notion of *people* implies the notion of sovereignty and there is only one sovereign in the Republic, and that is the French people.

The same controversy resumed in 2000 around a new plan for Corsica put forward by the government. Jean-Pierre Chevènement was once again in the forefront of the battle: to make his point, he resigned as Minister of the Interior to protest the government policy on Corsica. In response, Max Gallo, one of his close friends, said that today the main threat to France is not Jacobin centralism but social disorder. 'The danger,' he said, 'is not the seam that's too tight, but the tear.'

The Government of Judges

As I mentioned earlier, when the Constitutional Council recently overturned some bills passed by the Parliament, many people protested, blaming the judges for acting like politicians. Since their decisions were critical of the socialist government, they were accused by the left – as they were by the right when the government was a conservative one – of encroaching on the representatives' job, at the expense of the division of powers.

More generally, judges' increasing interference in political life, brought on by the many scandals involving politicians, has come under strong criticism for fostering a 'Republic of Judges.' This has been especially the case since all the political parties decided that as soon as one of their leaders is indicted, even though he will be presumed innocent, he will have to resign from his position as minister or as candidate to an election. According to the so-called republicans, the consequence of this situation is that French judges now hold a veto over who should be a minister, and who should resign, without any control from the people. The *judicialization* of public life has become a matter for concern in French political culture.

In the name of this culture, we cannot admit the idea that above the law, as it is passed by the Parliament, there can be a higher principle. This principle is what we call in French *le droit*. In French, we draw a distinction between *le droit*, which is the principle underlying the law, and *la loi*, which is the legislation itself. In English, the same word, *law*, is used for both concepts. For our republicans, there is no other law than the one passed by the legislature, and judges should not overturn it. It is the law of the people.

Of course, by *law* they mean the *state*. They complain about the decline of law, that is to say of authority and discipline. As one Republican critic wrote in a manifesto, 'when the law of the Republic vanishes, one must not be surprised to see the law of the jungle take its place.'

The School System

School, for the republicans, is the first pillar of the Republic. This is the place where individuals are stripped of their particular features, of all that links them to specific groups – ethnic groups, family groups, regional groups. In the name of equality, they are brought up to become French citizens. Being a citizen is what connects all Frenchmen beyond their social backgrounds, and the purpose of school is to forge those connections. At school they become French, instead of bourgeois or proletarians, Parisians or provincials, immigrants or natives. Citizenship is an abstract notion but it is also necessary to the unity of the Republic and to the expression of the general will. In the republican model, public school is the expression of equal opportunity; it aims to both instil the same values in all French children and to promote an elite.

It follows that teachers are the most important servants of the Republic – an idea that goes back to the Third Republic. French writer Charles Péguy glorified teachers in the well-known pages of his essay 'Money (L'Argent).' He called them the 'black hussars.' Under the Third Republic, what was expected from these teachers was assistance in uniting the French people.

The state is the symbol of this unity. Jules Ferry, the father of free, non-religious, compulsory instruction, said in 1880–1 in his famous letter to teachers: 'To make the Republic lovable is a national policy: you can, you must have it enter the minds of the young children.' And sociologist Emile Durkheim, an important figure in the Third Republic, explained: 'Education being a social function, the state cannot keep away from it. On the contrary, education must, in some way, depend on its action.' The school doctrine of the Third Republic was the legacy of the Jacobin discourse about 'regeneration' and the creation of a new mankind. Thanks to school, children were to be protected from the influence of families, of religion, and of the past.

The debate about schooling is a permanent one in France. It was relaunched some ten years ago in connection with the question of the Islamic scarf – whether Islamic schoolgirls should be allowed to wear a scarf to conceal their hair, as ordered by fundamentalists. The issue of the scarf was contested by two camps in France: those who, in the name of republican secularity, opposed the notion of girls displaying their religious or ethnic commitments, and those who advocated a more tolerant attitude.

The debate emerged again, in a different way, after Lionel Jospin became prime minister in 1997. This time it was with regard to the school policy of Claude Allègre, the Minister of Education, who was sharply attacked by teachers and eventually removed from his post. It pitted the republicans, who claimed to be the champions of 'knowledge,' against the democrats, who stood up for 'pedagogy.' According to the former, priority must be given to knowledge, which means that teachers must convey a common knowledge, the same for all, even if this knowledge may seem unfamiliar to some students. According to the latter, pedagogy must take precedence; the main question is how to get in touch with students, how to fill the cultural gap that is widening as enrolment becomes more democratic, how to start a dialogue between teachers and students, how to adapt teaching to students' levels and expectations.

One of those who continue to fuel this conflict is the French philosopher Régis Debray, who used to be a close aide to François Mitterrand after a much earlier career as a guerrilla in Che Guevara's army. In 1989, Debray published an article in the French magazine *Le Nouvel Observateur*, for the bicentenary of the French Revolution, titled 'Are You a Democrat or a Republican?' [2]Debray's analysis of republicans versus democrats was mentioned many times in the political debate. And indeed, it contains echoes of the antagonism in the United States between the Republican and Democratic parties, at least in regard to their origins. Roughly speaking, the American Republicans advocated a strong federal state, whereas the Democrats stood up for states' rights. Debray's thesis is based on a similar opposition, even though it refers to a different tradition.

In his piece, Debray describes two political behaviours, or two political representations – the republican one versus the democratic one – in a very sharp and striking way. What are the main differences between the Republic and democracy in Debray's eyes? Here are some of them.

The Republic worships the state, whereas democracy trusts society (what is called civil society as opposed to the state). 'In a Republic,' writes Debray, 'the state overhangs society; in a democracy, society dominates the state.' He adds: 'In a Republic each person identifies as a citizen and all the citizens constitute the nation; in a democracy each person identifies with his community and all the communities make up society.'

Debray also writes: 'In a Republic the state is free from any religious influence; in a democracy churches are free from any state influence.' And he goes on to say: 'In France the separation of churches and the state means that churches must give in to the state; in the United States it means that the state must give in to churches.' I could carry on with many other quotations. For instance: 'The Republic moderates the antagonism of interests and the disparity in conditions with the primacy of law, democracy deals with them through the pragmatic way of contract.'

And a quotation, which is important because it is about school: 'In a Republic society must resemble school, the first mission of which is to train citizens; in a democracy school must resemble society, its first mission being to train producers to have them adapted to the job marketplace.' In Debray's eyes the aim of the republican school is to free men from their environment; the aim of the democratic school is to make them fit it.

On one side – the republican one – you find such concepts as the state, public school, law, centralization, unity, the citizen, and the nation. On the other side – the democratic one – you find society (as opposed to the state), contract (as opposed to law), religion, decentralization, diversity (as opposed to unity), and communities (as opposed to the nation). On the one hand, public service; on the other, private interests. On the one hand, the *volonté générale*, inherited from Rousseau; on the other, the *volonté de tous* inherited from Montesquieu. On one side, priority given to equality; on the other, priority given to liberty.

This dichotomy may seem overstated. And I think it is. But it refers to the common republican myth as it is advocated by certain people in France today: the myth of a peaceful and united nation under the authority of the law, without any dispute and dissent; the myth of the general will that erases all differences and conflicts; the myth of the Golden Age or the lost paradise; and the myth of the time when order prevailed, when individuals as citizens merged into the national community, and when social unity was preserved by strong institutions.

The oversimplification of the republican myth substitutes the dream of unity for the analysis of the actual situation. This image can be traced back to Rousseau's work or, in the nineteenth century, to the work of the historian Jules Michelet. Michelet mentions those 'simple and extraordinary' words delivered to France by the City of Paris in 1793: 'We have only one desire: to get lost in the big whole.' Or, in another quotation from Michelet: 'Without unity we will perish.' Writer Benjamin Constant, who stands for another kind of Republic, thinks exactly the opposite: 'Diversity is life, uniformity is death.' In Debray's view Constant would be a democrat, not a republican. On the one hand you find those who emphasize the autonomy of individuals and who are not afraid of a divided society; on the other hand you find the will to merge individuals into a coherent and homogeneous society, the fear of schism and dissent, and the search for a common belief.

It is no surprise that most of the so-called republicans worry about the European Union, which, they say, may endanger France's characteristics and make it resemble the other European countries. They were opposed to the treaty of Maastricht – which established the Euro – because they regarded the national currency as a symbol of the national sovereignty. They believe the European Union will undermine France's independence and force France to adopt laws and practices at odds with its own traditions.

I am not suggesting that France give up all its specific features, but I think there are other ways of asserting one's own identity or, let's say, one's own values. It's high time we forgot about the republican myth, or at least seriously amended it. This myth accounts for a temporary form of the Republic, inherited from the Old Regime (the sovereignty of the king being merely transferred to the people), before it was strengthened by the Empire and adopted by the Third Republic. Today it produces negative effects.

As François Furet put it, there has been a decline of Jacobin political culture in France, that is to say, of the belief in the state as 'the key for social change.' Public opinion is still egalitarian, he explains, but it believes that 'its claim to equality does not require a Jacobin revolution any more nor state control on economy but is fulfilled through the idea of the rights of individuals, especially social rights.' According to Furet, the idea of the republican state as 'an arbiter and a protector' has lost all meaning.[3] I think the mission of the Republic in the twenty-first century will be to associate equality with individualism, unity with diversity, the sense of the nation with the sense of differences. The Jacobin Republic belongs to the past. It is really a myth – that is to say, an old story.

NOTES

1 Raoul Girardet, *Mythes et mythologies politiques* (Paris: Seuil, 1986; Points-Histoire, 1990)
2 Régis Debray, 'Etes-vous démocrate ou républicain ?' in *Le Nouvel Observateur*, 30 November 1989. Republished as 'République ou démocratie' in *Contretemps. Eloges des idéaux perdus* (Paris: Gallimard, Folio Actuel, 1992), 15–54.
3 François Furet, 'La France unie ...' in François Furet, Jacques Julliard, Pierre Rosenvallon, *La République du centre. La fin de l'exception française* (Paris: Calmann-Lévy, 1988), 15–66.

Russia's Babel: Myth Production and Its Purposes

ANDREAS HEINEMANN-GRÜDER

Since the demise of the Soviet Union and the refounding of the Russian state, Russia has been searching for self-images that connect the past to the present, address the desire for uniqueness, and provide mobilizing ideas. Most observers agree that post-Soviet Russia's search for a cohesive national identity has been futile,[1] but implications of this failed search are under dispute. Some authors claim that Russia's lack of a coherent national ideology was a major source of its misery in the 1990s. Others hold that the absence of a hegemonic nationalist ideology prevented a regression into authoritarianism. The absence of nationalist mass mobilization, successful nationalist parties, effective paramilitary groups, a Weimar Republic scenario, and large-scale interethnic strife is seen as a positive result of failed nation building, at least when we compare Russia with the former Yugoslavia.[2] Still others claim that Russia's liberals left the ideological field to chauvinists and in so doing allowed right-wing forces to fill the postsocialist ideological void.[3]

One theoretical and three explanatory questions arise from all this: First, what functions do national myths play in social cohesion? Second, what explains the sequence of temporarily prevailing national myths? Third, how are national self-images – images largely produced by intellectuals – linked to public self-perceptions? Fourth, what accounts for the multiplicity of national images instead of a single, cohesive, hegemonic one? I am not dealing with Russia as seen through Western eyes, though I am well aware that Russian positions are defined in a dialogue or heterologue with Europe and the United States.[4]

I call this paper 'Russia's Babel' because according to the Biblical story, a strong, unified voice was a prerequisite for constructing a tower that would reach the skies. God's answer to this human presumption was multilingualism, which prevents collective action. Should the Russians be content with God's punishment, or should they strive for a unified voice in order to reach the skies? In most assessments it is assumed that a 'normal' national idea should be a tangible, well thought out, well designed, and coherent given. But if we applied this criterion, no single nation-state would seem to present a national idea. Normality would exist only in the eye of the beholder. The contradiction between assumptions and observable reality should make us aware of a crucial distinction. Whenever we deal with Russia's national self-images, we should reflect on our normative assumptions on the one hand and explanations for what we observe on the other.

There is a fundamental hypothesis in social science that has a bearing on our judgment about Russia's national identity (or, for that matter, multiplicity of identifications). Stable state–society relations, the assumption holds, require a sense of loyalty, belonging, solidarity, commonality, and – to put it shortly – trust and diffuse support. There must be some emotive bonding among members of huge, anonymous communities if majority or state authority decisions is to be accepted, if life under one state authority is to have meaning, if a short-sighted instrumental approach to the state is to be prevented, if public support is to be mobilized. The assumption is that heterogeneous people need homogeneity in the form of shared goals and a shared culture. Wherever broad support for political authority is lacking, politics will end in authoritarianism or fragmentation. It is usually the task of shared and well thought out conceptions of nationhood to provide trust and support. Nonetheless, the claim that diffuse support is necessary provokes more questions than it provides answers. On what grounds could and should these overarching conceptions emerge? Isn't the claim for an essentialist national identity simply the takeover of nationalist fundamentalism by social scientists?

Functions of National Myths

Let me state my own basic assumptions regarding the role of national myths in bonding society with statehood. National bonding is, in my understanding, a process of active identification that occurs in three contexts: intragroup relations, group–state relations, and insider–outsider relations. Identification with a national group is not objective in any academic sense; rather, it is driven by interests in identification. The coherence of national self-images (or lack thereof) thus expresses degrees of shared interests. National commitments are always group related; they are a permanent collective process of construction. It follows that the content of national myths develops and changes over time. Mythologies, *logos* of identification, clichés about self and others, standardized habits of social behaviour – all such expressions of commonality – fulfil basic functions for group cohesion. Myths produce archetypical images of a collective self, of its desires, fears, and dreams.[5] National communities are constantly developing repertoires of identification that are strongly heterogeneous and often competing. The temporary prevalence of a hegemonic discourse depends on context, actor configurations, and interests.[6] Political actors employ various identities at the same time. Nonetheless, repertoires of national self-definition are rather limited. Because of their normative, communicative, and coordinating functions, the core ideas of self are repetitive, standardized, and easily recognized and identified. The ultimate contraction of the repertoire, the successful suppression of competing identifications, could be interpreted as the epitome of nationalism; in contrast, the openness of the repertoire to democratic deliberation limits the discourse only in one respect: the fundamental rules of the discourse itself are secured against easy change.

When signifiers of recognition are created, the costs of communication are reduced, knowledge is pooled, and the reaching of agreements is made easier. Codes of bonding also instil a sense of shared interests and provide a sense of comfort. As a result, the group's status may be preserved or increased and the potential success of the group may be furthered.[7] To carry out these functions, national commitments depend on coordination. The most important media of co-ordination are nationalist ideologies, a stylized view of history, and political leaders who offer commonsense epistemology. Political leaders thus play a key role in creating group commitment through their power to channel and coordinate communication as well as through their power to sanction defection from group patterns. From the state's perspective, the main goals are to secure loyalty to its authority and to mobilize the public for political aims. Given the variety of possible group identifications the state has a compelling interest in securing a hegemonic position in the discourse in order to reduce the repertoire and to control the openness of the public space. In order to secure loyalty to state authority, national norms thus require reinforcement through the continued reiteration that defection may well result in lost comforts and opportunities. National myths further define insider–outsider relationships by setting rules for inclusion and exclusion. National norms are therefore highly particularistic. The in-group norms give preference to national members. Myths of inclusion and exclusion, often formalized as norms, claim spaces for exclusive national decision-making power, instil a sense of uniqueness, and provide privileged access to resources.

It follows from these general observations that national group cohesion can be built on various grounds. In each individual case it will exhibit a unique mixture of ethnic and civic, of religious and secular elements, as well as backward-looking and forward-looking legitimizations. Fragmented and heterogeneous national identifications are a fairly normal phenomenon. Yet countries vary in their degrees of national coherence; much depends on which stage of nation building they are at and on the strength of common interests.

The Postsocialist Condition

Before turning to the question of what characterizes the Russian national discourse, let me highlight some common causes of nationalism in post-socialist settings. The end of socialism coincided – admittedly to different degrees – with the breakdown of crucial state institutions. The state's capacity to provide public services eroded, social insecurity became rampant, the former apparatus of repression lost its efficiency, and inefficient and non-responsive institutions were often unable – at least in the early stages of transformation – to channel the concerns of minorities. All of this resulted in discontinuity, fragmentation, loss, and confusion.[8] The state's often continuing control of the mass media helped channel discomfort into ethnic mobilization. The deliberate distortion of information about others was possible as long as the mass media were controlled.

Besides these structural conditions, ideological legacies and the peculiarities inherent in coming to terms with the hardships of transformation played into the hands of nationalists. For example, stereotypes of socialist authoritarianism and of nationalism show remarkable parallels. An authoritarian style of decision making, an antagonistic, imperialist, and militaristic style of thinking, a messianic ideology, a cult of leaders combined with a cult of masses, antiliberalism, and an aversion to compromise are all common features of both the socialist mindset and the nationalist one. In Russia's case one could add that Stalinism – with its national Bolshevism, repression of non-Russians, superiority complex, and constant search for internal enemies – provided mental maps on which post-Soviet nationalists could build. Russia's lack of an outright process of de-Stalinization may explain why campaigns against Jews and people from the Caucasus still play such a prominent role in the consciousness of the masses.

Furthermore, nationalism proved to be a useful means of coming to terms with the socialist past. Myths of victimization, long harboured and newly reactivated, became specific means of denying subjecthood under socialism. This is why almost all eastern Europeans are now competing for exclusive rights to victim status. Alleged victims of historical injustice feel sufficiently legitimized by their self-ascribed victimhood. Adherence to a national victim group prevents empathy for other national groups; it also reduces self-perception to the constant contemplation of received wounds. It has been widely observed that the establishment of a 'civil society' in late socialism quite often took a national form. But the idea of 'civil society' was always more a means to criticize communist rule than it ever was a conceptualization of democratic society. Rhetorics of sovereignty were resorting to the ideological legitimization of communists – socialism as the people's power – while turning it against its originators. Popular sovereignty was translated into ethnic sovereignty, but this did not necessarily add up to a civil society.

The Repertoire of Russian National Ideologies

You can find in Russia (as well as in Western assessments) a widely held, cyclically resurfacing opinion that Russia lacks a civil society and significant traditions of liberal and democratic thinking. It is therefore doomed to autocracy, unable to overcome its historic deficiencies and to mature.[9] Russians are said to be authoritarian-minded, dependent on state leadership, and – because of the imperial and Orthodox Christian legacy – patriarchic and state-centred in their mindset. Culture serves as the favoured explanation for explaining Russia's flaws in democratization. But is Russia's culture as coherent as we generally assume? Why is it that Ivan the Terrible in the sixteenth century is made to bear responsibility for Yeltsin's and Putin's styles of governing? There is at least an explanatory gap.

The repertoire of national ideologies is actually not as homogeneous as often proclaimed. Authors who argue that Russia has a dominant authoritarian tradition find it difficult to explain the emergence of *perestroika*, Gorbachev's passionate talk of the common European house, grassroots movements and the mushrooming of non-governmental organizations, liberal thinking at the end of the 1980s and the first years of the 1990s, and the wide array of liberal legislation that has been enacted since Russia's independence.[10] Obviously, the repertoire of ideas that politicians can mobilize is much broader than is supposed by deterministic claims. Yet it is nonetheless striking that in Russia's case all the key elements in the national discourse were already present in the nineteenth century. Post-Soviet Russia was not very inventive in this respect.

Here I offer a working typology of Russia's competing and at times incompatible national ideologies, while acknowledging that the lines between the camps are often blurred: liberal westernizers, Eurasianists, romantic Slavophiles, and statists.[11] In terms of cultural insider–outsider relationships, Russia has mostly related itself to Europe.[12] Russia's image of the United States during the Cold War and after reflected a desire to be recognized as a Great Power rather than an attraction to America's culture and political system. For the Russian state, Europe served as the dominant defining Other. Even those who deny Russia is part of Europe define that nation in European terms. Never in Asian terms, because when it comes to Asia, Russians across the ideological board have always seen themselves as a European civilizing force. The images of Europe reflect two things: an idealized projection of what Russia should strive for; or, on the contrary, an image of what is dangerous to Russia's uniqueness.

Liberal westernizers traditionally embrace a pro-European view and see Russia as part of an enlightened European civilization, alienated from this natural belonging by Stalinism, the Cold War, and reactionary forces in Russia's history. The liberal camp clearly dominated the second half of the 1980s and the first years of the 1990s. Former dissidents, adherents of Gorbachev's *perestroika*, and the post-Soviet economic liberals can be grouped into this camp. With respect to society–state relations, liberals emphasized human rights and a liberal economy. Russia should, according to this thinking, integrate with the West, develop the ingredients of democracy, and abstain from an ethnic definition of the nation. Russia should represent a multiethnic and multicultural state. Some liberals – the so-called Atlanticists – place more emphasis on cooperation with the United States, whereas others see Western Europe as the natural partner. The heyday of Europeanization was of course Gorbachev's *perestroika*, with its new thinking in foreign policy and its call for a pan-European house. The Soviet Union,

Gorbachev proclaimed, was an organic part of broader European history.[13] Initially, Yeltsin and his young entourage adhered to a similar and even more radical liberal position, one of great optimism regarding Russia's rejoining of European civilization. Liberals prevailed in Russia's executive until 1993. They could rally societal support on the basis of their strong anticommunist credentials and their highly utopian promises.

Liberal ideas failed in Russia for two reasons. The first is that passivity, lethargy, and a deadening sense of fatality were *de facto* treated as positive assets of system change. Reform-minded elites could push privatization as long as the public (i.e., the civil society) remained passive. Russian liberals embraced individual rights but did not like the public to get involved and organized. Regional legislatures and the Duma were kept powerless and incentives for party formation remained weak. The liberals harboured an inherent distrust of the people. The second is that post-*perestroika* liberals and their ideological competitors did not engage in public discourse regarding how to build on democratic traditions, or regarding Russia's European legacy. Instead, the liberals were characterized by their anticommunism and by their selective absorption of national rhetoric; they had no concept of a civil society. A law-based, democratic, accountable, and constitutionally bound government did not rank high on the agenda of liberal, promarket parties and politicians. Recent evidence of the liberals' failure can be seen in their silence about the war in Chechnya.

Initially, even Russia's communists had opted for Russia's sovereignty; even so, the dissolution of the Soviet Union was keenly felt as the demise of Russia's status in the world. Russia's newly elected president, Boris Yeltsin, had played a decisive role in dissolving the USSR, and this provoked a search for the guilty. The corrupt government and economic hardships such as hyperinflation and the nonpayment of pensions and salaries disillusioned many Russians in regard to liberalism and democracy. In polls conducted in the 1990s, abstract democratic values prevailed over a return to the past or authoritarian rule, but disappointment in the results of liberal reforms was rampant.[14]

A partial explanation for the demise of the liberal strand can be found in its own conception. In terms of domestic policies, the liberals were usually silent. They were antistatist and anti-isolationist, but they did not develop a positive image of a future polity. Russia's liberals – with the notable exception of the Yabloko Party – did not conceptualize democracy as based on an active citizenry, strong special-interest groups, a vibrant party system, and public discourse. To legitimize their approach they adopted anticommunism, an almost Bolshevist revolutionary attitude, and an ideological belief in the economic imperatives of system change. As long as Yeltsin held power, the liberals preferred to concentrate power in the executive and did not spend much time thinking about political institutions and democratic traditions in Russia's history that could have been used to mobilize democratic support – for example, the Zemstvo movement, federalist thinking in the nineteenth century, and human rights activism among former dissidents. Liberals based their approach on the myth that Russia is part of the West. The crisis of liberalism was answered by one of three possible myths: Russia as a bridge; Russia as an enigma; and Russia as sheer state power.

Criticism of the liberal approach blamed the reformers not only for being selfish but also for serving as agents of outside powers. In the discourse of nonliberal ideologies, two strands that had already emerged under Gorbachev gained ground: Eurasianism and romantic Slavophilia. The Eurasianist strand in Russian thinking, with its strong roots in the philosophies of the 1920s and 1930s, sees Russia as a bridge between Europe and Asia. Eurasianism never highlighted Russia's 'Asianness'; emphasis was placed instead on Russia being an equal partner of Europe, not simply a part of it. Eurasianism, in its historical version and also in its contemporary one, articulates Russian fears of having to follow European blueprints of capitalism and European military order.[15] Russia, in order not to be swallowed or colonized by Europe, should seek allies in Asia. The Eurasianists argue that Russia should not 'apprentice' itself to the West, as the liberals argued; rather, it should be a partner of the West.[16] One could characterize this kind of nationalism as protectionist, as that of potential losers.

Among contemporary Eurasianists we find many former liberals who wish to copy European models – especially social democratic ones – but not at a breakneck pace. The dynamism of Europe is not dismissed: what is rejected is a normative, economic, or military hegemony over Russia. The notion that Russia must live up to Europeans' expectations is strongly rejected. Furthermore, contemporary Eurasianist positions try to draw a distinction between Russia and its Central and Eastern European neighbours, who claim to be 'returning to Europe.' Eurasianism is thus mainly oriented toward sovereignty in foreign policy, with no specific claims in the domestic realm. The Eurasianist position is highly ambiguous, in a kind of love-hate relationship with

Europe, which is seen as the most desired as well as the most feared model. Contemporary Eurasianism exposes most of the romantic, spiritual, and antirationalist traits of its predecessors. Compared to its classic representatives, such as Nikolay Trubetskoy and Nikolay Berdyaev, who have embraced the German conservative critique of liberalism (Arnold Spengler, Carl Schmitt, Karl Haushofer), recent Eurasianism's primary target is Atlanticism, which emphasizes the alleged monopolar dominance by the United States and which advocates geopolitical striving for anti-American partners in Europe (primarily Germany), Asia (China, India, Japan), and the Middle East (Iran).[17] Contemporary Eurasianism aims to keep the 'amoral' and 'individualistic' American role models at bay, but without actually proposing alternative Russian models for civic society, state–society relations, and state–economy interaction.[18] While abstractly embracing an egalitarian and communal ethos, Eurasianism *de facto* confines itself to the following causes: denying Western individualism as alien to Russian culture; exalting Russia's imperial grandeur; and championing images of strong state power. Historically, Eurasianism tried, as Boris Ponomarev put it, 'to reconcile the Slavophile premise about Russia's unique historical destiny with the Bolshevik's emphasis on a strong state.'[19] After the dissolution of the Soviet Union, these older commonalities allowed Communist leaders such as Gennadiy Zyuganov to replace Soviet internationalism with Eurasianist isolationism as part of their post-Soviet ideology.[20]

Romantic Slavophiles are even more fond than the Eurasianists of the myth that Russia is surrounded by Russophobic enemies. Non-liberal nationalist ideologies have adopted self-victimization as their main theme. Russians have often been blamed by non-Russian ethnic groups of the former Soviet Union for the October Revolution, the imposition of Soviet rule, Stalinism, and imperial attitudes, but Slavophiles refuse outright to pay the bill for the legacies of Soviet history. Slavophiles want the Russians to be seen as victims of Soviet rule too, even greater victims than the rest. Obviously, this has led to conflict, the result of which has been politics that emphasize differences rather than shared experiences. The claim to victim status has helped externalize responsibilities for the past. Totalitarianism, the externalizing argument holds, was imported from Western Europe, and thus had Hegelian roots, not Russian ones. Socialism, it is claimed, had no roots at all in Russian history before the nineteenth century, when it was imported from Germany.[21] Slavophiles combine harsh critiques of Western liberalism, America, ecological devastation, and 'technocracy' with a cult of nativism, an admiration for the 'wise' and 'true' people, and sympathy for the plight of the Russian peasantry. Furthermore, Slavophile ideas often include anti-Semitic prejudices. Active involvement in politics is discouraged in favour of a high moral ground, one with strongly spiritual connotations. Slavophile themes have ranked high among prominent Soviet dissident writers, especially Solzhenitsyn and the writers of 'village prose' (the most outstanding example being Valentin Rasputin).[22] After the dissolution of the Soviet Union, Slavophiles who had originally denounced communism as alien to Russia often found common ground with nationalist communists; the two shared an anti-Western attitude and a disrespect for individual human rights.

A popular theme among romantic Slavophiles is doom saying in the best tradition of Soviet Slavophile dissidence. Socialism and especially Stalinism, it is said, depleted the intellectual and moral gene pool of Russia. Talk of genocide against Russians is common, and conveys three messages: ultimate victimhood, helplessness, and a desperate call for collective survival instincts. In the face of extinction, all disputes should be forgotten. Salvation rests in miracles to come. Romantic Slavophiles are responding to a perceived repression of Russianness, to marginalization pressures, and to an alleged imposition of homogeneity in the form of Western political, cultural, and economic models.

Romantic Slavophiles love to portray Russia as a mystery that Westeners cannot comprehend. The goal of this mystification is simple: to reject Enlightenment and rationality and to protect Russians from intellectual intercourse with non-Russians. But mystification does much more than this: it protects against self-reflection. At the core of romantic Slavophilia we find the rejection of egoistic utilitarianism, the glorification of the peasant community (*obshina*), suspicion of private property, the dismissal of formal laws, the worship of the state as a saviour, spiritual arrogance, and claims to a national 'essence.' The genuine Russian nation is conceived in an organic sense. Russian history is scoured for moral inspiration on themes such as heroism, self-sacrifice, communalism, social harmony, the depth of the Russian soul, and romantic images of the countryside. The romantic quest for an 'essentialist' Russian identity makes all Russians equal and buttresses claims to a distinctive type of civilization. Yet the romantic negation of Europe and the West is not based on an elaborate non-Western value system. Unlike Confucianism, Islam, and Hinduism, it is based more on negation than on any original conception.

Adherents to the 'Russian Idea' like to speak in the name of the people in very abstract and idealized terms. The people are treated as a lodestone for moral inspiration but not as an empirical entity. Slightly adapting a famous saying by Dostoyevsky, romantic Slavophiles love the Russian people but hate each individual. In Russia's romantic nationalism, xenophobic, pan-Slavic, and anti-Semitic themes are often mixed. Compared to the liberal, Eurasian, and statist versions, romantic Slavophilia is the most ethnicized ideology in the Russian repertoire. It claims a Russian uniformity that denies individual and social interests. Romantic Slavophilia is the strongest form of resistance against a necessary transformation of identities, and in that sense is essentially antimodern and antidemocratic. Instead of narrowing the gap between Russia's political and economic realities and its self-image, romantic nationalists oversimplify Russia's complexities with their claims that stressful parts of reality are a result of the non-Russian world's encroachments.

Russia's values are repeated again and again in order to instil a sense of in-group loyalty that claims precedence over internal differences. Russia's romantic nationalists use myths of the 'Russian Idea' to trump regional attachments, religion, class affiliation, economic self-interest, cosmopolitanism, gender, and so on.[23] In this way, the tensions between a putatively homogeneous integral identity and plural, cross-cutting identities are suppressed. Through equalization rather than social differentiation, the romantic nationalists aim to assert the essential Russian identity. Russia may be poor, but its soul is far richer than that of the selfish West. Perestroika, liberalism, and a pro-Western orientation are criticized as alien to the Russian soul, and the proponents of these things (most prominently Gorbachev) are regularly portrayed as traitors and as agents in a Western plot. It is supposed that Russia and Europe belong to different, even opposite cultures. Under this rubric, romantic nationalism incorporates forces that otherwise would be strongly heterogeneous. Communists blame Gorbachev for betraying them, but so do former dissidents like Solzhenytsin, and even hardline chauvinists like the writer Prokhanov.

A common feature of all ideological strands is the conception of Russia in polarized terms, in antagonistic 'either/or' choices: either Western or not, either democratic or authoritarian, either liberal or statist, either spiritual or enlightened, either state or society oriented, seeking either harmony or fragmentation. Romantic nationalism is well documented and a special focus of Western research; but in all the major conflicts of the 1990s – the fate of the Russian diaspora, territorial disputes with former Soviet republics, conflicts with autonomous republics within Russia – romantic nationalism has not attracted significant mass support. Rather, it has remained a largely intellectual exercise.

Statist nationalism is the latest brand of Russian national ideology, and under Vladimir Putin it is now not just the official ideology, but the only one being marketed. The Russian government claims on its Web page that Russia does not possess the same long liberal traditions as the United States and United Kingdom. For Russians, it is said, a strong state is not something to be overcome. Rather, it is a guarantee of order, a source of and engine for change.[24] Statism worships the authority of the presidency without relating it to functions to be fulfilled, apart from those of law and order. Against the backdrop of widespread moral decay, the state as the main source of this decay is declared to be the solution. Unlike Eurasianism and romantic nationalism, statism rejects claims to moral superiority over the West, and it does not seek to mystify the Russian soul; unlike liberalism, it refuses to commit itself to rapid modernization. It is even hard to discern any meaning in this ideology, apart from the Hegelian admiration of state authority, which is inherently close to despotism. Putin did not publish an electoral platform and he refused to participate in campaign debates. Consequently, it is hard to judge what the substance of this statism is going to be. Nonetheless, statism also produces its own mythology – the fantasy of salvation by a strong state and leader, and the presumed and inherently antiliberal and antirepublican belief that state authority should and can constitute society. In all likelihood, Russian-style statism will increase the power of bureaucracies, ministries, the police, and the agencies that regulate the economy. These facets of the state will strengthen their control over grassroots organizations and the liberal mass media. It is still too early to judge whether Putin will produce any tangible results in fighting corruption, insider trading, and the illegal transfer of capital – all the problems of Russian transformation, most of them generated by the state's bureaucracies themselves. In terms of insider–outsider relationships, Russian statism is likely to widen the chasm in values between Russia and Europe, and to pursue at very least protectionist if not outright isolationist policies. In terms of state–society relations, the republican and liberal idea of limited government and empowerment of society is being replaced by its opposite. Statism that worships a strong leader does not address the problem of feeble state–society relations – for example, the lack of institutionalized participation in, and transparent channels of access to, the political process for the different elements of society.

The contraction of the ideological repertoire in Russia around statist and Eurasian positions is fostering authoritarianism and a hardening of borders to the West, for domestic integrative purposes. The statist position runs counter to liberal as well as active civic society conceptions and is thus likely to intensify the disempowerment of societal actors. After six years of a corrupt and handicapped presidency in decay, Putin is the first leader to garner some respectable degree of support. But his support is based on people growing tired of defeatism, rather than on the active embrace of a program or the adherence to a party with a program. It was the war in Chechnya, not some new, mobilizing political concept, that become the government's means to project some aura of efficiency, credibility, and law-and-order competence. By pointing at the Chechnyans as the culprit, the government was able to externalize the distrust that people had in it. A lasting integrative and bonding effect is unlikely to emerge from all of this. The declamation of strong statehood has not yet provided any means for integrating and accommodating diverse interests in lasting coalitions. The shrinking of the repertoire furthermore mirrors a perceived cutting off of alternatives, such as inclusion in Europe.[25]

Mass Perceptions

How can we explain the fact that ethnic issues have not dominated the electoral preferences of Russians? Obviously, common socialization on ethnocultural grounds has lost its integrating power for forming group identity. Recent studies on Russia's diaspora in the Near Abroad demonstrate that identification on ethnic grounds is largely dependent on context: ethnic identity is only retained where benefits can be expected; where not, assimilation takes place.[26] Economic deregulation and the plurality of lifestyles have led to differentiation and individualization, clearly dividing younger cohorts from Soviet-socialized ones.

Russian identities feature a growing nostalgia for the past, a denial of obligations to the state, and mostly non-ethnic characteristics of Russianness. The number of those regretting the dissolution of the Soviet Union grew in the 1990s, to 76 per cent in 1999. Almost two-thirds (65 per cent) think that Russia has enemies, with Western financial circles, NATO, and the United States dominating the list.[27] There is a widely shared belief in a Western plot and a betrayal, but only 2 per cent of respondents polled in 1996 were prepared to unite in order to counter the West.[28] The longing for a strong state – 71 per cent expect the state to ensure the well-being of each citizen – is striking but highly ambiguous. According to a 1996 poll, only 20 per cent recognized the priority of law, while 72 per cent said they would abide by the law if officials did the same.[29] Yuri Levada summarizes it this way: 'The relationship with the state is seen as one of mutual cheating.'[30] The state is somehow abstractly perceived as a bearer of justice and equity, but not of law. A strong state should care about basics such as paying pensions, providing jobs, securing public order, and delivering food. Yet at the same time, the yearning for a strong state is not identical with a quest for totalitarianism: 70 per cent of the respondents in 1996 asked for a strong leader, 56 per cent for democratic procedures, and 88 per cent actually wanted a lawful society.[31] With respect to how Russians describe their personal qualities, attributes such as 'hospitable,' 'open and assuming,' 'patient,' 'ready to help,' and 'hard working' feature high, whereas 'religious' and 'cultured' feature low.[32] In polls conducted in 1996, only a minority claimed ethnic superiority.[33]

When we compare the calls for Russian greatness with public perceptions, it is obvious that the diffusion of internal tensions through a quest for external grandeur has only partly worked out. The image of the West has significantly deteriorated, yet Levada rightly observes:

> The argument of 'imperial grandeur' singularly fails to strike a cord in the Russian people. It works neither in promoting the interests of the center, nor in promoting order in the provinces. State economic goals fare no better ... A far more primitive factor proved to be immeasurably more powerful in raising support for the recent action in Chechnya: fear ... This fear combined with such pat sentiments as outrage over 'Western interference,' shame of receiving Western aid, and anger about 'dominance of Caucasians' in Moscow's markets.[34]

When we relate the ideological repertoire to the elections in the 1990s, we see a sequence of dividing lines. In 1991, with Yeltsin's first election to the presidency, the vote was in favour of Russian independence and democracy and against the Soviet centre. The organizing 'other' was socialism Soviet-style, neither another nation, nor Europe, nor the United States. In the 1993 Duma elections, Vladimir Zhirinovsky's Liberal Democratic Party of Russia got almost one-quarter of the vote. But except for these elections, insider–outsider relationships never arose as a dominant theme in electoral campaigns. Intellectual debates about a Russian identity did not take hold among the masses. Even attempts by Zhirinovsky and by the Moscow mayor, Luzhkov, to rally Russians around the fate of Russians in the Near Abroad did not find public appeal. As a rough summary of the shift of dominant discourses in the 1990s, we can say that in the first half of the decade antistatist, liberal positions prevailed, and in the second half state capacities advanced as the major theme. After nationalist and communist forces achieved a rapprochement, the liberal project was challenged by quests for a strong state and for social protection, and by a longing for past imperial greatness. In 1996, anticommunism was back as the major divide (Yeltsin against Zyuganov), very likely for the last time. In ideological terms, the first postsocialist Duma elections took place in 1999. Neither national nor ideological themes prevailed; rather, the focus was on state performance, corruption, crime, and relations between the centre and the regions. Even the ongoing Chechnyan war did not cause either nationalist mobilization or a liberal critique. Instead, the Chechnyan war reflected a quest for a central state based more on order and competence than on nationalist emotions.

Reasons for the Lack of a Hegemonic National Idea

Applying Miroslav Hroch's phases of nationalist mobilization, Russia's nationalist strivings remain stuck between stage A (elaboration of ideas) and stage B (concerted agitation), and have never reached stage C (serious mass mobilization).[35] Contemporary Russia resembles a language without a grammar. Russians struggle to communicate, but the sounds are without if–then connections. Some authors have even gone so far as to label the lack of appropriate language as aphasia[36] – a state of loss of speech. The mystification of Russia may actually represent nothing more than a lack of intelligible speech. What explanations can be offered? Obviously, the loss of the tsarist and Soviet empires did not lead directly to the birth of a Russian nation-state. Russia's exit from past role patterns seems more protracted than in some Central and Eastern European countries. It appears to be stuck in anachronistic role models and to be unable to envision post-Soviet role alternatives. Key features of the Soviet past are still cherished by neocommunists, chauvinists, and religious nationalists alike: the great power status, the addiction to negativism[37] (mainly directed at Western liberalism and pluralism), and the worshipping of state power (derzhavnost) and collectivism (sobornost) instead of individualism.

In scholarly literature, most blame for the problem of role exit is placed on Russia's historical legacy.[38] The imperial self-perception embodied in tsarism as well as in Soviet rule,[39] the unclear physical extent of Russia,[40] the state-centred rather than community-based self-images, the supra-national claims of the Orthodox Church, the unclear delineation of the Russian ethnos from Slavophile conceptions,[41] the absence of a deeply rooted civil society, and the undermining of key aspects of Russian national tradition under Soviet rule are all treated as factors that have done much to determine post-Soviet self-images.[42] The strong residues of the past are nonetheless highly contradictory – more expressions of symbolic integration than rallying cries for mass mobilization – and this casts doubts on culturalist assertions of overdetermination. The stated speechlessness may actually reflect doubts about role commitments. Most Russians see the adoption of a post-Soviet identity as an abrupt, imposed, and chaotic departure from the Soviet past rather than an expression of deliberate preparation and free will. The vast majority of Russians would have preferred to preserve the Soviet Union, and the marginalization of Russia and Russians following the dissolution of the Soviet Union is not perceived as a voluntary role exit.

Yet the traumatic impact of lost imperial status does not fully explain the holdover identity derived from the previous status.[43] Obviously, a backward-looking, anticommunist legitimacy did not prove sufficient for rallying support behind system change. But the same holds true for romantic and chauvinist nationalism. Cynical pragmatism and the absence of ideological divides characterize the contemporary Russian spirit. Since the failure of Gorbachev's social democratic concept and Yeltsin's early liberal concept, no new mobilizing idea for state–society and state–economy relations has emerged.[44] In highlighting the lack of social bearers of nationalism in Russia, it is also useful to adopt a structural rather than an ideological point of view. The absence of differentiated and organized social and corporate interest groups could be seen as an impediment to overarching community cohesion. The heterogeneity of national identifications may reflect a lack of shared interests. The formation of parties, associations, and social groups is still very fluid, and the common, overarching ground is respectively thin. The variety of identifications would thus reflect the particularistic interests of an early stage of social differentiation.

Special attention is often paid to the peculiar role played by Russia's intelligentsia. It is claimed that the Russian intelligentsia is dead, pauperized, diminished in its status with regard to the people it speaks of (but rarely likes to be identified with).[45] Evidently, the intelligentsia is economically on the same level as the people (*narod*) it worships but does not like to belong to. In socialism, the Russian intelligentsia had been a small breed, self-indulgent, complaining, telling jokes and fairy tales, and mistaking the reading of good books for social responsibility. In contrast to Adam Michnik and Jacek Kuron (Poland), Vaclav Havel (Czechoslovakia), and Georgy Konrad (Hungary), Russia's intelligentsia has indulged in inner migration and backward-looking idealization instead of becoming a moral authority for a vibrant civil society. If we relate the intellectual revival of the 'Russian Idea' to post-Soviet experiences, the gap between image and reality could not be wider. This backward-looking romanticism invites psychological and social explanations. If intellectual imagination is almost totally disconnected from reality, it may demonstrate only one thing: the ideology of an intelligentsia encapsulating itself in martyrdom. The lack of civic virtues in Russia's intellectual discourses could be explained by the intelligentsia's benign role in system change. Russia's liberal intelligentsia, instead of tapping grassroots support and playing a key role in liberalizing late socialism, has – with notable exceptions such as Andrey Sakharov and Sergey Kovalyov – been either state conformist or merely backward-looking. Historians usually play a key role in forming a shared epistemology, and the absence of a strong dissident tradition in Soviet historiography and the prevalence of former Marxism-Leninism instructors among Russia's myth producers may explain why ideas of the nineteenth century figure so prominently in contemporary myth production.[46] Furthermore, the absence of de-Stalinization in public discourses allowed for the preservation of at least some of the traits that Stalinism shared with the romantic nationalism of the nineteenth century: moral absolutism, a rejection of the West, and worship of Russia's status as an empire. In a sense, former Marxist-Leninist historians simply switched from one software to another, using the same MS-Soviet operating platform.

Russia entered the postideological age without ideological parties. Thus it lacks the social bearers of traditional ideological party formation. It has no working class movement, no religious movement, no liberal middle class, and no territorial party system. Instead of parties as intermediaries between society and government, the country is dominated by temporary and pragmatic blocs that are keen only to be in power. There are two quasi-program parties, embracing extreme right and left forces: the LDPR and the Communists. But in many respects, even the Communists and the now defunct LDPR are more client-oriented than program parties. The majoritarian and exclusive features of Russia's political regime discouraged the emergence of a party system with cross-cutting cleavages and requirements for coalition building. Whereas nationalism mobilizes the masses, the Russian political regime disempowers parties. Because of its bias toward concentrating power in the executive, Russia's political system did not produce incentives for working coalitions. Russia's institutional choices in the 1990s – low inclusiveness, few channels for interest aggregation – may thus have reinforced older patterns of state-centrism.

Conclusion

In Russia's case, the historical repertoire for choices of identity is rather limited. Looking at the sequence of dominant myths, we discern a strong inter-relationship: subsequent models build on the negation and flaws of prior models. Each new model is a kind of antimodel to the former, but none is a post-Soviet model *sui generis*. The ideas tested thus far have neither provided an idea for Russia's future shape nor mobilized civic society toward shared goals. The sequence of dominant national identities reflects the fluid interests of state leaders and political elites. The fact that backward-looking ideas did not grasp the 'masses' indicates that Russia is no longer a traditional, agrarian society. Instead, Russia's society is educated, urban, and mobile; it is also subject to a variety of offers for a post-Soviet identity. Russia seems stuck between dysfunctional, anachronistic role models and a still distant idea of a community of citizens based on positive identification with the constitutional order and the political system.

Fortunately, what holds true for civic identity affects nationalism as well. Ethnocentric nationalism has proved a weak source of mobilization.[47] The dominant rallying cry in Russia is not the politics of ethnicity, but rather a quest for state capacity. Given the imperial self-image, the most urgent task seems to be to adjust role models to suit actual capacities.

The fragmentation of the national repertoire under conditions of weak adherence to rules results in a state of unpredictability, of not knowing where to go. The fragmentation of Russian society is only weakly regulated by rule of law, not to speak of a civic identity and an adherence to political institutions based on positive experience. Egoistic, individualistic gain-maximizing behaviour should not therefore be surprising. Yet certain commonalities must have prevented a total state of anarchy. Further research will have to consider whether Russian-language patriotism, cultural pride in Russian literature, wide acceptance of Russian as the *lingua franca*, a high degree of ethnic homogeneity, and a diffuse acceptance of Russia's constitution helped mitigate disruptive tendencies.

What seems to be most needed is a discourse related to the problems Russia is facing in the twenty-first century. In the end, Russia is not going to resemble any European nation-state, so repeated complaints about Russia's lack of national identity are moot. It would seem more appropriate to organize discourses on the efficiency of governance and civic legitimacy instead of demanding that Russia repeat nation-building classes it missed in the nineteenth century.

NOTES

1 Anatol Lieven, 'The Weakness of Russian Nationalism,' *Survival* 41, no. 2 (1999): 53–70; Gerhard Simon, 'Rußländische Nation: Fiktion oder Rettung für Rußland?' *Berichte des Bundesinstituts für ostwissenschaftliche und internationale Studien* 11 (1999).

2 Lieven, 'The Weakness,' 53f.

3 Yitzak Brudny, *Reinventing Russia* (Cambridge: Harvard University Press, 1998), 264f.

4 Martin Malia, *Russia under Western Eyes: From the Bronze Horseman to the Lenin Mausoleum* (Cambridge: Harvard University Press, 1999).

5 C.G. Jung, *Bewußtes und Unbewußtes* (Frankfurt am Main: Fischer, Beiträge zur Psychologie, 1957), 13; Carl-Friedrich Geyer, *Mythos: Formen, Beispiele, Deutungen* (Munich: Beck 1996).

6 Alexander Wendt, 'Anarchy Is What States Makes of It: The Social Construction of Power Politics,' *International Organization* 46 (1992), 405.

7 These insights draw upon Russel Hardin, *One for All: The Logic of Group Conflict* (Princeton: Princeton University Press, 1995).

8 This section draws partially on Vladimir Tismaneanu, *Fantasies of Salvation: Democracy, Nationalism, and Myth in Post-Communist Europe* (Princeton, NJ: Princeton University Press, 1998), 3–22.

9 Tim MacDaniel, *The Agony of the Russian Idea* (Princeton: Princeton University Press, 1996), 13.

10 Nicolai Petro, *The Rebirth of Russian Democracy: An Interpretation of Political Culture* (Cambridge and London: Harvard University Press, 1995).

11 Vera Tolz suggested a different typology: imperial 'resurrectionists,' slavophile 'Great Russians,' and ethnocentrists; see 'Conflicting "Home-

land Myths" and Nation-State Building in Postcommunist Russia,' *Slavic Review* 57, no. 2 (1998): 268 and 289ff.

12 Boris Groys, *Die Erfindung Rußlands* (Munich and Vienna: Carl Hanser Verlag, 1995).

13 Iver B. Neumann, *Russia and the Idea of Europe* (London and New York: Routledge, 1996), 162.

14 Yuri Levada, 'Homo Sovieticus Ten Years On,' *Russia on Russia* 2 (June 2000): 13–28.

15 See the collection of classic essays on Eurasianism in I.A. Isaev, ed., *Puti Evrazii: Russkaya intelligentsiya i sud'by Rossii* (Moscow: Russkaza Kniga, 1992). A recent call for Eurasianism is represented in Aleksandr Dugin, *Osnovy Geopolitiki* (Moscow: Arktogeya Centr, 1999). The former dissident Lev N. Gumilev provides a 'biogeographical' justification for setting Russia apart from Europe, see L.N. Gumilev, *Etnosfera: Istoriya lyudey i istoriya prirody* (Moscow: Ekopros, 1993). Gumilev, relying on ideas of Johann Gottfried Herder without ever making a reference, claims that Russia's habits are determined by its landscape. On the impact of Eurasianist ideas on Russia's foreign policy see Jens Fischer, *Eurasismus: Eine Option russischer Außenpolitik?* (Berlin: Berlin Verlag Arno Spitz, 1998).

16 Neumann, *Russia and the Idea*, 200.

17 Dugin, *Osnovy*, 777ff.

18 The Spenglerian critique of Western decadence is taken up by the Russian communists, too. See A. James Gregor, 'Fascism and the New Russian Nationalism,' *Communist and Post-communist Studies* 31, no. 1 (1998): 1–15.

19 Boris M. Ponomarev, 'Historical Culture,' in *Russian Culture at the Crossroads: Paradoxes of Postcommunist Consciousness*, edited by Dmitri Shalin (Boulder, CO: Westview Press 1996), 20.

20 Ponomarev, 'Historical Culture,' at 29, writes: 'Calls to restore the Russian empire to its past glory are coming from such diverse personages as the neo-Slavophile Rasputin, the communist Gennady Zyuganov, and the statist (*derzhavnik*) Aleksandr Prokhanov, and it is highly indicative that these diverse thinkers and groups invoke Eurasianist arguments to justify their demands.'

21 Neumann, *Russia and the Idea*, 171.

22 Valentin Rasputin, *Farewell to Matyora: A Novel* (Evanston, 16: Northwestern University Press, 1995); Aleksandr Isaevich Solzhenitsyn and Yermolai Solzhenitsyn, *The Russian Question at the End of the Twentieth Century* (New York: Farrar Straus Giroux, 1995).

23 A collection of historical sources on the 'Russian Idea' is to be found in M.A. Maslin, ed., *Russkaya Ideya* (Moscow: Izdatel'stvo Respublika, 1992);

for an interpretative account, see Bettina Sieber, 1998, *'Russische Idee' und Identität. 'Philosophisches Erbe' und Selbstthematisierung der Russen in der öffentlichen Diskussion, 1985–1995* (Bochum: Projekt Verlag, 1998).

24 www.pravitelstvo.gov.ru.

25 NATO extensions have sent a clear message: Russia does not fit into the West.

26 David Laitin, *Identity in Formation: The Russian-Speaking Minority in the Near Abroad* (Ithaca: Cornell University Press, 1998).

27 If not indicated otherwise, the data given are based on VCIOM polls mainly conducted in 1989, 1994, and 1999, as documented in 'The Fate of Homo Sovieticus,' *Russia on Russia* 2 (June 2000).

28 The data are quoted from Elena Chinyaeva, 'The Search for the Russian Idea,' *Transition* 4, no. 1 (1997): 43ff.

29 *Ibid.*

30 Levada, *Homo Sovieticus*, 21.

31 Chinyayeva, *The Search*, 42.

32 Levada, *Homo Sovieticus*, 21.

33 Thirteen per cent of those questioned by the Independent Institute of Social and Nationalities Problems in February 1996, cited after Chinyayeva, *The Search*, 42.

34 Levada, 'Patience and Protest,' in 'The Fate of Homo Sovieticus,' *Russia on Russia* 2 (June 2000): 36.

35 Miroslav Hroch *Social Preconditions of National Revival in Europe: A Comparative Analysis of the Social Composition of Patriotic Groups among the Smaller European Nations* (Cambridge: Cambridge University Press, 1985).

36 Sergei A. Oushakine, 'In the State of Post-Soviet Aphasia' (unpublished paper, Columbia University, 1999).

37 Moshe Lewin, *Russia/USSR/Russia: The Drive and Drift of a Superstate* (New York: New Press 1995), 302f.

38 Ronald Grigor Suny, *The Revenge of the Past: Nationalism, Revolution, and the Collapse of the Soviet Union* (Cambridge: Cambridge University Press, 1994).

39 Geoffrey Hosking, *Russia: People and Empire, 1552–1917* (Cambridge: Harvard University Press, 1997).

40 Wendy Slater, 'Russia's Imagined History: Visions of the Soviet Past and the New "Russian Idea,"' *Journal of Communist Studies and Transition Politics* 14, no. 4 (1998): 69–86.

41 Sven Gunnar Simonsen, 'Raising "The Russian Question," Ethnicity and Statehood – Russkie and Rossiya, *Nationalism and Ethnic Politics* 2, no. 1 (1996): 91–110.

42 Lieven, *The Weakness*, 54f.

43 On stages of role exit see Helen Rose Fuchs Ebaugh, *Becoming an Ex: The Process of Role Exit* (Chicago and London: University of Chicago Press, 1988), esp. 181ff.

44 After Yeltsin's reelection in 1996, a commission was set up, led by Georgiy Satarov, to develop a new national idea, but no concept was ever delivered.

45 Masha Gessen, *Dead Again: The Russian Intellgentsia after Communism* (London and New York: Verso, 1997).

46 A representative collection of essays by former Marxism-Leninism instructors turned Russophiles is to be found in Yu. S. Kukushkin, ed., *Russkiy narod: istoricheskaya sud'ba v XX veke* (Moscow: Izdatel'stvo ANKO, 1993).

47 If we look at national identities in post-Soviet states, strong ethno-nationalism at the cost of civic inclusiveness inhibited democratization and stimulated ethnic conflict. See Ronald Grigor Suny, 'Provisional Stabilities: The Politics of Identities in Post-Soviet Eurasia,' *International Security* 24, no. 3 (1999/2000): 139–78.

Foundation Myths and the Reflection of History in Modern Hungary

LÁSZLÓ KONTLER

It is common sense that myths of origin play a crucial role in the formation of national consciousness and identity. This paper reflects on the state of collective historical memory in Hungary as it is expressed in attitudes towards the foundation of the medieval kingdom of Hungary by Stephen I and the Revolution of 1848. Most people's attitudes towards these two watershed events – one marking the beginning of Hungary as a territorially organized community, the other often taken to symbolically represent the beginning of Hungary as a modern nation – reflect their status as historical myths – that is, as the basis of convictions widely held within the community that strengthen the ties holding it together, and as episodes closely related to major moments in past experience (albeit in several aspects barely standing the test of historical criticism). The views advanced below reflect the reasons why I published a book on the history of Hungary[1] a year ago: to write a short 'history of Hungary without tears,' as a Canadian friend has put it. I will argue that the currently widespread infatuation with the first event (1000) and the relative indifference toward the later event (1848) can be explained in light of Hungarians' tendency to view their national history in tragic and pessimistic terms, and that all of this is highly relevant to the Hungarian historical consciousness in its present form.

Speaking on 'Culture, Community and Nation: Scotland at Home and Abroad,'[2] Tom Nairn argued that frustration at the loss of political independence through the 1707 Anglo-Scottish Union not only bred a certain parochialism among Scots, but also made them 'world-class experts in nostalgia,' cultivating a national image firmly stuck in a glorious past. Alluding to the coming devolution, Nairn was modestly optimistic about the future. Nevertheless, he emphasized that the Scots have always seen their national history as as a proclaimed tragedy, as a glorious struggle in which David always loses to Goliath.[3]

It may not be obvious, but Nairn's claims have a specific relevance to my theme. A sense of *déjà vu* immediately struck me while I was reading an account of his lecture. Hungarians are well known, not least to themselves, for looking back on their past with almost unbearable heartbreak, for perceiving their nation as having been robbed of its greatness by cruel events. Some of these events have played a role in the great drama of history, in which Hungarians have all too often been rendered helpless outsiders, playing the part of the small nation struggling valiantly and successfully against the odds. Just like the Scots. I have watched Scots giving up their alleged reluctance to take it easy when it comes to sensitive points of their history. Last spring, at Stirling Castle, I witnessed a small historical re-enactment of the ancient martial arts of the clans. About a dozen valiant Highlanders appeared on the lawn of the courtyard, heavy swords in hand, thick beards and colourful kilts blowing in the wind. 'Anyone from England here?' roared the strongest of them. As soon as some cautious 'yeas' were uttered, instantly the cohort, swords swinging, charged in their direction with a mighty *hooray*. (All Englishmen survived the charge.) Could the same thing happen, I asked myself, if the scene were an old fortress in Transdanubia (not too many of which still exist: the Habsburgs had most of them blown up after suppressing the War of Independence led by Prince Ferenc Rákóczi in the early eighteenth century), if the Highlanders were replaced by Hungarians dressed as the 'outlaws' led by Imre Thököly or Rákóczi's *kuruc* soldiers, and the Englishmen by a bunch of tourists from Austria? Hardly, I'm afraid. In our corner of the world, national history is still supposed to be a matter of pathos and dignity; irony of this kind is considered disgraceful.

Hungarians' view of their national past – one that is still all too common among them – is perhaps reflected most closely in their national anthem. The lyrics are based on a poem by Ferenc Kölcsey, written in 1823 at the beginning of the national awakening; in 1844, at the height of the nationalistic fervour, the music was composed by Ferenc Erkel. The Hungarian nation, whom 'ill fate that has torn for ages,' has 'already suffered the doom of times past and future' and therefore deserves a 'merry season' at last. All of this clearly reflects the attitudes I am referring to. Roughly a century after the anthem was written, those same attitudes underpinned the words of Gyula Illyés, lyricist, novelist, and national icon, from 1938:

Hungarians ... owe their existence to their audacious struggles. These struggles have been defensive fights from the beginning and became increasingly desperate as they went by. All hopeless. Surprisingly enough, these are the most hopeless at the moment they are launched: the enemy is always at least twenty times stronger, and sober minds would avoid such a venture. The nation, famous for its calm and objective way of thinking, is aware that its venture can only end in failure, but still, time and again it attacks Goliath. Our forebodings always prove right, but we never learn from the lesson. Our history does not teach us logic. It teaches us, and this is comforting and lofty, that things such as courage, audacity and insistence on ideas also have value in the life of nations. It is only by miracles that people can live thousands of years, by the example of the phoenix.

This translation of Illyés's words (which sound more noble and somewhat less pathos-ridden in the original) appears as the cover blurb of *The Illustrated History of Hungary*, published last year,[4] a generally excellent and beautifully produced volume that nevertheless occasionally reflects that same spirit which also imbues the lines of the venerated poet. As a final illustration of my point, let me refer to a speech by Hungary's Minister for the National Cultural Heritage, made to a large international audience at the 1999 Frankfurt Book Fair, on the occasion of Hungary being the 'focal theme' of that event. Much of what the minister had to say about Hungarians' history and identity, and the interrelatedness of these, fit comfortably into the stereotypical straitjacket of a small nation suffering under the blows of adversity and yet even under such circumstances making laudable contributions to European civilization.

After a perhaps overlong introduction, let me explain why I feel this simplistic interpretation of Hungarian history is inadequate. All stereotypes contain a grain of truth – sometimes much more than a grain. Adversity there was, and a lot of it, and the contributions, too, have been remarkable. But when we distill this into the perspective outlined above, we run the risk of concealing what is truly meaningful in the nation's heritage in the twenty-first century, of establishing false priorities and thereby precluding a responsible and realistic manner of coming to terms with the national past. Without question, Hungary has survived many periods of severe adversity. Consequently, it is all too easy and comforting for Hungarians to persuade themselves that whatever glory there was is their own achievement, and that whatever is unpleasant to remember has been imposed on them. I would like to illustrate this point by describing the changing attitudes to the two watersheds in Hungarian history mentioned earlier and by explaining how they relate to this kind of reflection of national history.

Surely the perceived hardships explain to a great extent the gloom that surrounds the interpretation of history which prevails both in public discourse and among Hungarians generally. To some extent these hardships excuse the sentimental notion of a small but heroic and morally superior people perpetually victimized through the schemes and the power games of others (be they the Ottomans, or the Austrians, or the Entente governments and their Slovak, Serb, or Romanian protégés, or the Germans, or the Soviets). They explain and excuse, but they do not warrant it. All three ingredients that are essential for a sound grasp of history, and consequently a sound national consciousness, are missing from this perception. These ingredients are realism, responsibility, and a sense of proportion. First, the view of Hungarian history of which Illyés's attitudes are a hallmark – a view that according to the testimony of the minister's Frankfurt speech is still popular today – is parochial and introverted: it lacks a sense of proportion in that it fails to ask whether Hungarian history is truly unique on account of the glory and the suffering, and whether it is in these elements that the uniqueness of Hungarian history truly consists. The horizon from which history is viewed must be broadened: everyone is unique, but it is in the uniqueness of others that one may properly recognize one's own. Second, if a community is to take its fate in its own hands and keep it there, in its collective memory it must be able to delineate very clearly its own responsibility for its past fortunes and misfortunes. If it fails in this exercise, or even tries to avoid the task, it is very likely, as I hope to show, to make false value judgments about the past and therefore to select improperly those traditions which could be relevant for the future.

The pessimistic or 'gloom and doom' perception and 'escapist' attitudes have been part of Hungarian history ever since the sixteenth century, when the country's fortunes began their steady decline, a result of domestic social and political crises aggravated by the Ottoman Conquest. The first tribulations at the hands of the 'infidels' took place at the same time as the rapid spread of the Reformation in Hungary, so at first, Hungarians took some comfort from Protestant eschatology: supposedly, they were God's chosen people whose steadfastness was being put to test by an uncommon plight; however, if they showed firmness in their belief, their Babylonian captivity, just like that of the

Jews, would come to an end. Ideas of elect nationhood[5] were sustained into the seventeenth century, when it seemed that (Protestant) Hungary was wedged between 'two pagans,' one of which – the Habsburg court, armed with the Catholic Counter-Reformation – seemed as formidable as the Ottomans. By the time the latter were driven from the country, Hungarians had been forced to realize that although for nearly two centuries they had thought of themselves as 'the bulwark of Christendom,' on account of their conflict with the Habsburgs (who in the end coordinated the campaigns that drove the Turks out of the country) many in Christian Europe in fact saw Hungary as an *enemy* of Christendom.[6] To be sure, this view eventually faded away, but only to be replaced by its variant, according to which Hungary was 'Eastern,' in the sense it later came to be seen in Western Europe. The latter, a product of the Enlightenment, reflected changing dichotomies in symbolic geography brought about by the fact that by the eighteenth century, Rome, Florence, and Venice had been replaced by London, Amsterdam, and Paris as Europe's centres of finance and culture. As a result, the former division into the refined South and the rustic North was replaced by one in which an affluent, sophisticated and civilized West was juxtaposed with the East, seen as barren and backward, populated by a barbarous peasantry and a hidebound nobility.[7]

To say the least, during the eighteenth century this view of Hungary was not entirely out of touch with reality: given the circumstances, it would have been surprising if that view had not emerged. This was recognized by the Hungarians themselves, and as a result, the view of the Hungarian predicament – based on the notions of glory, plight, and what I have called escapism – began to emerge in full armour in this period. The nobility's staunch insistence on their privileges was conceived of as ardour for the liberties of the nation. By the standards of the time, this was not entirely posturing: the *natio Hungarica* was perceived as consisting only of the *nati*, the 'natives' of the houses with a pedigree – that is, the nobility whose interest was, it followed, the national interest. Also, by vigorously defending the estates-based 'constitution' (to be more precise, the traditional customs and statutes of the realm) and thus ensuring the continued survival of deliberative assemblies and organs of self-government on the municipal as well as the national level, they were maintaining an important political tradition that could be tapped in later years. However, this was achieved at a serious cost. Elsewhere in the Habsburg lands, under Maria Theresa, the nobility, however grudgingly, abandoned their tax privileges; in Hungary, however, they resisted all attempts to make them contribute to state revenues. Though their insistence on maintaining the entire network of rural relations connected with their privileges, the nobility played a major role in perpetuating the country's backwardness. They were, of course, aware of this, but they threw all blame at the door of Vienna, which supposedly was pursuing colonial policies toward Hungary. The pattern was set: for most of the eighteenth and early nineteenth centuries, Hungarian parliaments attributed the country's dismal conditions to political oppression and to economic exploitation by Austria. These grievances were not entirely without basis: the imperial administration could not but think in imperial terms, and it did its best to strengthen the 'established branches' of the economy. As a consequence, Hungarian industries were dwarfed by their Austrian and Bohemian counterparts. Furthermore, the Austrians made every effort to prevent Hungarian agricultural products from being exported to the western half of the Habsburg Monarchy. Yet it is doubtful whether different policies would had resulted in a rosier general picture; also, it is certain that the stubborn insistence of the Hungarian estates on their *gravamina* and their refusal to address domestic causes of stagnation did little to stimulate soul searching and critical thinking.

It would be grossly unfair not to add immediately that when the unsustainability of the old regime was first recognized, that recognition came from the sons of the enlightened nobility, both its aristocratic and gentry segments. This realization on their part inaugurated the period during which a critical reflection of Hungary's condition and history was more readily observable than ever before or, sorry to say, since. The Age of Enlightenment came to its fullest flowering in Hungary when it was acknowledged that the number one cause of Hungary's backwardness is not her subordination to Vienna, but the feudal system. The way to emerge from that system was not through a quest for erstwhile glory, but by polishing the human mind and the human environment and by forging a sense of community, a *societas civilis* where there had been only an assemblage of groups of subjects possessing highly diverse rights and privileges. Gergely Berzeviczy, perhaps the brightest of the gentleman political economists who came to intellectual maturity under Joseph II, was the first to point out, at the turn of the eighteenth and nineteenth centuries, the indigenous roots of backwardness, using the most up-to-date statistical methods. His labour inevitably pointed to the urgent need to take stock of and pass judgment on an immense and complex web of customs, statutes, attitudes, and interpersonal relationships handed down through many centuries.[8] Regarding the character of the protagonists of Hungarian history, the nobleman was perceived as valiant and chivalrous and as sharing the quality of honesty with his antagonist, the peasant; but both were also equally notorious for their diffidence and for lack of enterprise. How did these less attractive and, what is more, less respectable qualities arise? From legal arrangements made as long ago as the mid-fourteenth century. The inalienability of noble lands had once served the purpose of preventing the fragmentation of noble estates, thus ensuring the survival of the line; but among the conditions of modernity it made the nobleman an impossible partner for banks, to which he could not offer security on loans contracted. So wrote Count István Széchenyi in his 1830 book with the highly appropriate title *Credit*.[9] The nobles lacked ambition because of their overdeveloped sense of entitlement; the same character fault among the peasants could be explained by statutes also deriving from 1351. Still in force at the time when Széchenyi was writing, these statutes provided nobles near absolute authority over their serfs and standardized their duties; the result was a peasantry suffering from economic misery and a lack of legal rights.

With these and other, similarly acute insights, Széchenyi's book and program brought about a shift in the entire discourse on Hungary's past and current predicament. The role of the foreign powers in Hungary's plight was not forgotten, but the overall picture was far better balanced; historical and public awareness improved in Hungary in the following two decades more than in any comparable period and perhaps reached its all-time peak. Merely on this account, the Age of Reform and its apotheosis, 1848, would be worthy of our attention. But more than that, a realistic and responsible assessment of Hungary's heritage and condition also produced the powerful vision of a future Hungary erected on the foundation of the 'reconciliation of interests': one in which the elite would no longer be segregated by legal privilege from the rest of the population, who would thus be 'lifted within the bulwarks of the constitution' (formerly strictly the property of the nobles); one in which the nation would cease to be divided through differences in legal status and became a 'society' in the truest sense of the word.[10] In these ways it was a republican program, not mainly with regard to the form of government (although in the heat of the War of Independence the overthrow of the Habsburgs was proclaimed) but rather in its advocacy of public spirit and civic virtue. It was also a liberal program, and some of its aims would be satisfied, and others rendered obsolete or insufficient, in the subsequent 140 years (for example, the serfs would be emancipated and the guilds abolished). Other elements of the program, such as representative government and civil liberties, were only temporarily and/or incompletely implemented until the reforms of 1989–90. Finally, this program was the work of the most talented generation of daring and committed leaders, who combined intellectual sophistication with political activism and a broad vision. Besides Széchenyi and his more radical counterpart, the chief political leader of 1848–9, Lajos Kossuth, there was the jurist Ferenc Deák, later the architect of the 1867 Compromise with Austria. There was also József Eötvös, a writer and political theorist of (in hindsight) European stature. And there were many others.

These features should have been more than sufficient to make 1848 *the* Hungarian historical myth suited to modern times. However, this 'cabinet of all talents' – a comparison with Charles James Fox's post-1806 British administration, to which this epithet was first applied, is by no means far-fetched – committed a sin that seems to have been unpardonable in the judgment of collective memory: they failed. The Compromise of 1867 may well have been a 'realistic' result of 1848, in that it secured parliamentary government, civil liberties, and autonomy in domestic affairs; but it was also, especially keeping the post-1867 developments in mind – the obstinate conservatism of the political system, the failure to embrace social reform, and especially the rampant nationality problem – a somewhat diluted one. This failure, and the reasons for it, had a lasting impact on public perceptions – in particular, on the public's evaluation of the 1848 revolution.

First, a theory of foreign domination, conspiracy, and treachery emerged: it has been suggested that the revolution failed because the military superiority of the Habsburg and Russian forces (an undoubted first cause) was strengthened by the malicious conniving (also capable of demonstration) whereby Vienna fomented rebellion by other nationalities against the Hungarian government and the Commander-in-Chief Artúr Görgey became a traitor. In fact, though Görgey had serious differences with Kossuth, he was a loyal soldier of the revolution and surrendered in August 1849 in an impossible military situation.[11] As to the nationalities, even without the overtures from Vienna (of which there were indeed plenty), they had already been explicitly unhappy for some time with the Hungarian liberals' idea of the 'unitary political nation' – with the notion that since each individual citizen should be entitled to enjoy the same civil liberties, claims to group autonomy were unnecessary and unwarranted; in other words, once individual rights became accessible to them, the ethnic minorities, just like the peasants,[12] would quickly assimilate into the new Hungarian nation. But the sentiments of the poet of the revolution, Sándor Petőfi, who Magyarized his name from Petrovics (Petrović), were not shared by everyone, and the revolutionary government's inevitable deafness to the claims of the nationalities until it was relatively late would have resulted in extremely violent ethnic strife even without the interference of the Habsburg court. (Somewhat similar is the case of the peasantry, whose expectations during those troubled times were not fulfilled as quickly as it had hoped, and who became increasingly passive – a fact often emphasized in Marxist interpretations as an illustration of the alleged narrow-minded class bias of the liberal nobility that led the revolution.) Nevertheless, in Hungarians' assessments of 1848–9, external evil has not merely overshadowed (which could be understood) but effectively annulled any mention of internal tensions. For instance, generations of high school graduates hardly realized that there *was* savage interethnic violence in Hungary in 1848–9.

Second, those achievements of 1848 which were not reasserted in 1867 may seem, in retrospect, as 'not vindicated by history,' and therefore as secondary in importance to the nation's heritage. Most key issues (representative and responsible government, civil liberties, etc. – peasant emancipation had already been implemented in 1851) received treatment in 1867 similar to that of nearly two decades before. What was sifted out was a part of the revolutionary spirit. Revolutionary euphoria, as always, implied some radical excess, but in the case of 1848 Hungary it was much more indicative of the aspirations (if not the realities) of social solidarity, which were impossible to recreate with the experience of the intervening two decades in mind: brutal suppression, retaliation in 1849–50, a system labelled 'neo-absolutism' in the 1850s, and then the negotiation of a settlement in a completely unrevolutionary situation after that.

Third, the status of 1848 was rendered uncertain by its failure: 15 March could never become 14 July. How was one to enshrine, in a nation obsessed with its perceptions of historical victimhood, the memory of such failure? The year 1848 became an object of veneration and lamentation at the same time, but it offered no reason for celebration. Thus, despite the best intentions, it has become undervalued and has fallen prey to the nation's general tendency to contemplate its history in terms of patriotic pathos.

During the dualist period, 1848 was remembered and 15 March celebrated as a symbol of national independence and as an occasion for voicing petty grievances against Vienna, but not as an opportunity to express the idea of social solidarity, which was at least as important a component in the heritage of the Reform Age and of 1848. Imperfectly expressed and even less perfectly executed at that time, this solidarity was nevertheless – or rather all the more – worthy of being maintained, rejuvenated, and further developed. Needless to say, 1848 and all it stood for could not have been a cherished memory in the national climate that emerged between 1914 and 1920, which saw the collapse of historic Hungary in warfare, postwar chaos (the abortive effort to create a democratic republic, which was followed by a Bolshevik coup), and a difficult peace. The circumstances of defeat and dismemberment were all but in favour, first, of historical realism and responsibility and, second, of progressive traditions. The process of disintegration stemmed overwhelmingly from internal causes, but because it culminated in a grossly unfair application of the principles of Wilsonism by the victors at the Paris Peace Conference – that is, an external event – a sober assessment of that disintegration was impossible. Whatever soul searching there was placed the blame squarely on the liberals and democrats, who had sapped the vigour of old Hungary and had thus caused it to fall prey to the nationalist aspirations of its neighbours and of Bolshevik internationalists.[13] Beyond that, all responsibility was assigned to the grossly unfair peace treaty. It goes without saying that in this way the peace treaty also contributed to the survival of precisely those semifeudal structures whose demolition should have been the main result of the whole transition process. Significantly, in the interwar period, 1848 as a symbol was only suitable for being placed on the banner of a (rather ephemeral) opposition movement, the March Front, launched in 1937 to urge measures against the spread of Nazism and to campaign for democracy, land reform, and cooperation with neighbouring peoples.

To be sure, 1848 did not fare much better under communism. This time, instead of being ignored or repudiated, it was at first expropriated and adjusted to the ideological needs of the regime, embedded in a fictitious tradition of working-class revolutionary radicalism whose apogee – so it was argued – was the current communist revolution. Curiously enough, the 'traitor' theory survived, and was adjusted to reflect the view that 1848–9 had been a class war rather than an independence struggle. Not even Kossuth, the revolutionary hero *par excel-*

lence, had been vigilant enough to prevent the class enemy from infiltrating the ranks of revolutionaries.[14] This constituted a warning to the 'heirs of the revolutionary tradition': it was supposed that 1848 represented the first, uncertain steps, the 1919 Soviet Republic an intermediate stage, and 1945 the true breakthrough. This alleged continuity was cemented in the 1960s into the wonderful idea of 'revolutionary youth days': a sequence of collective commemorations under the aegis of the Communist Youth League, on 15 March, 19 March (the anniversary of the 1919 Bolshevik takeover), and 4 April ('Liberation Day,' i.e., the day the Soviets expelled the Germans in 1945). Then, in the mid-1970s, each spring grim-looking colleagues from the municipal party cells were sent out to high schools for discussions with the 'revolutionary youth' and to place a special emphasis on the fact that of these dates, 4 April was the greatest national holiday, whatever anybody might agitate to the contrary. This measure was a response to the resurgence of 1848 as an opposition symbol and 15 March as an opposition holiday. The first 'alternative commemoration' in 1973, emphasizing the national and liberal democratic character of 1848, resulted in beatings and detentions and was followed by several years of silence; but it was revived by the budding opposition to the Kádár regime in the 1980s. These peaceful and by no means huge protest rallies regularly ended in the same fashion as the one in 1973 – until 1989. That year, 15 March was perhaps the most visible sign of a sea change. As one of the very few mass movements during the transition in Hungary, the march that day of about 100,000 people in central Budapest sent the clear message that many of the one-and-a-half-century-old endeavours were still unfinished and that it was time to put them back on the agenda.

One year later, in March 1990, free elections took place in Hungary. It seemed that the moment of truth for 1848 might finally have come. During the previous three decades the 'soft dictatorship' associated with Hungary's post-1956 leader János Kádár – which offered relatively greater material welfare and private autonomy in return for political equanimity – had had a compromising and extremely harmful effect on the remnants of civic commitment in Hungary. For optimists, it seemed only logical that once this quagmire had been crossed, one important tradition of Hungarian history – that which focused on social solidarity, public awareness, and rational spirit – would become paramount. But this did not happen. When asked what the greatest Hungarian national holiday is – and, by implication, what is the most decisive component of the national heritage, the standard by which they wish to be measured – well over 50 per cent of Hungarians today say it is 20 August (with 15 March coming second with 20-odd per cent, somewhat ahead of 23 October, marking the Revolution of 1956, and, still, 4 April).

I have not yet mentioned 20 August. That is the day on which, in 1083, the earthly remains of Stephen I were removed from the stone casket in which they had rested for forty-five years and placed in a silver chest as part of the canonization ceremony of the king who founded the Hungarian monarchy and converted its people to Christianity.[15] That day is the holiday of Saint Stephen, and by implication the holiday of the foundation of the Kingdom of Hungary (even though Stephen's coronation took place either on Christmas Day in 1000 or on New Year's Day in 1001). Incidentally, it is also the holiday of the 'new bread,' the first bake from the current year's grain harvest. I might also add that as Hungary's communist constitution was issued on the same day in 1949, by way of an ironic transubstantiation the holy king's day was for decades celebrated as 'Constitution Day.'

The foundation of the medieval monarchy (usually referred to nowadays as the foundation of the state – quite imprecisely, given the fact that this term did not obtain its present meaning before early modern times) was obviously a landmark in the history of Hungary. But as the same event was arguably no less important in the history of any other nation, the quite unparalleled status of it in Hungarians' collective memory and public remembrance requires an explanation. After all, in spite of François Furet and other revisionist historians, the French celebrate 14 July and not Hugh Capet or Charlemagne or Clovis. For the United States, the fact that 4 July stands for sovereignty and democracy saves the dilemma, while the English, reputed to cherish their traditions, commemorate neither Alfred the Great nor William the Conqueror nor the Bill of Rights with an ardour equal to the Hungarian infatuation with 20 August, Saint Stephen, and the relics associated with him – the most important one being the Holy Crown.

One of the clues – perhaps the one most often given in public discourse – is that these objects of infatuation symbolize Hungarians' capacity for survival and testify to the bravery and persistence with which the nation has always maintained 'statehood' (another anachronism) in one form or another. This merit was praised, oddly enough (but from personal experience), by Emperor and King Francis Joseph, who emerged as the ruler of the Habsburg inheritance in the troubled winter of 1848, at the millennium of the Hungarian conquest of the Carpathian Basin. But if we look beyond the Carpathians, we must realize immediately that from the north through the west to the south-west, Stephen's coronation was being witnessed by peoples – Poles, Czechs, Austrians, Croats – who were also establishing or had already established themselves in the region and who have since then survived an equal number of equally troubled centuries.

Next, the creation of sovereignty – yet another notion that did not exist until Jean Bodin made it the focus of his theory of the polity in the late sixteenth century – for its own sake is made out to be a reason to celebrate. There are two problems with this. First, the dimensions – not the fact – of celebrating the creation of monarchical sovereignty a thousand years ago are out of proportion with the realities of a republican constitution today. We are told that the Holy Crown of Saint Stephen – which, being an assemblage of two crowns from the late eleventh and the twelfth centuries, our first king never wore – has symbolized through the centuries not kingly rule, but rather Hungarian 'statehood.' This is a problematic assertion nowadays. It is true that when, in the early and mid fifteenth century, unruly baronial factions held kings under control, they claimed to govern the country 'under the seal of the Holy Crown,' which represented the community of the kingdom. But this was a community of the privileged: just as with the *natio Hungarica*, mentioned earlier, the theory of the Holy Crown was based on exclusiveness and did not regard commoners as members of the political body. In the early nineteenth century the veneration of the crown came into fashion again on the initiative of the Habsburgs, as an alternative to revolutionary cults modelled after French ones. It was Deák in 1861, who first referred to the crown as the symbol of the lands of Saint Stephen. However, this usage did not become truly widespread until the interwar years, when political semantics invested it with a very specific meaning – as a touchstone of bitterness over the Trianon Peace Treaty. If it is added that the veneration of relics – which in our case also include Stephen's miraculously preserved Holy Right Hand – is not acceptable for Protestants, yet another dimension of exclusiveness in the cult of the Holy Crown becomes discernible. For all that, no effort has been made to adjust the tradition of the Holy Crown to the requirements of a society based – I hope – on tolerance and mutual understanding. The mere assertion that it represents Hungarian 'statehood' is questionable; the strengthening of this assertion through the ceremonial transfer of the Holy Crown from the Hungarian National Museum to the House of Parliament, which took place on New Year's Day in 2000 (the 999th anniversary of Stephen's coronation) is not fully convincing. It would have been delightful if the masterminds of this move had made it clear that the transfer was intended to *establish a new tradition*, one meant to build a bridge between Hungary's ancient, monarchical past and its parliamentary present. (It could have been asked, though, why the Parliament, which had a dubious record from the late nineteenth and early twentieth centuries, was a better symbol of modern Hungary than the National Museum, which was founded in the early nineteenth century precisely to mark Hungary's efforts at national, social, and political emancipation.) This did not happen: instead, the *maintenance of old* tradition was emphasized, clumsily and with little credibility.

Summa summarum, supposing that Hungarians are at least somewhat aware of these ironies, then regardless of what they claim, 'sovereignty' in itself cannot explain their attachment to 20 August. All the more so – and this is my second point relating to 'sovereignty' – as it is not very difficult to provide an iconoclastic (not to say sacrilegious) reading of 'Stephen's creation.' The hagiographical story that Stephen refused a crown offered by Emperor Otto III in order to avoid taking an oath of fealty, and that he accepted the insignia sent by Pope Sylvester II, has long been proved apocryphal[16] (although it does not cease to be recalled again and again: I last encountered it in the New Year's issue of a leading Hungarian daily, in a survey of Hungary's thousand-year history by the winner of the high school pupils' national prize for history[17]). The years around 1000 were a rare moment in history when the ambitions of the local rulers in Central Europe coincided with the agreement of the pope and the emperor on a 'project' of expanding the *respublica Christiana* eastwards. The coronation of the new rulers in the region took place with the endorsement of both – it could hardly have been otherwise. Stephen's 'creation' took place, with the very active involvement of Roman priests and bishops and German knights, at an enormous cost in terms of ancient customs, traditions, and human lives. Sovereignty? Before he indeed rid himself of foreign tutelage (during the latter half of his reign), Stephen had initially established his authority against rebellious Hungarian chieftains by relying heavily on foreign support. It may well be that another often quoted and grossly misinterpreted statement of his refers to this experience. In his admonitions to his son Prince Emeric, Stephen warned that monolingual *regni* are weak and therefore immigrants should be welcome. This has been interpreted as an early token of the Hungarians' well-known hospitality and general tolerance – another part of Stephen's legend (I last read it mentioned in an interview around 20 August 2000, by both the freshly elected Hungarian president and the Minister of Justice). I do not believe that the Hungarian national character is any less hospitable than any other. Alas, *regnum* in this particular case should be taken to mean not kingdom or country, but the king's retinue – in which foreign knights indeed rendered Stephen great service.[18]

So what we have here as 'Stephen's creation' – and the aspect of it that elicits admiration – can be described in avowedly anachronistic terms as a magisterial exercise of reason of state, an uncommon act of efficient statesmanship. (It is noteworthy that when his canonization was pushed through by Ladislas I, it was not even pretended that Stephen's piety accounted for it: his 'saintliness' consisted in converting his people, and it was not concealed that serious violence had been involved in this process.) And this statesmanship was so successfully performed that it laid the foundations of some sort of power standing for Hungary during the first five centuries of its existence – something that it then lost, subsequently thought it had regained at the end of the nineteenth century, and finally lost again, this time forever. In 1920, Hungary changed from being a medium-ranking state of over 20 million – in dreams fuelled by the experience of peace, progress and prosperity at the *fin-de-siècle*, even 30 million – to a small nation of 7.5 million, with limitations on its sovereign status, but with a historical consciousness still corresponding to the earlier situation. This left an indelible mark on that consciousness. If the recovery of the lands of Saint Stephen is only urged by an insignificant minority in Hungary today, the successful acts of power performed by him, so conspicuously missing from our modern history, fascinate a far greater number (many of whom are also undoubtedly confirmed in their sentiments by the religious revival that has taken place since the fall of communism – after all, the cult of Stephen is to a considerable extent a religious cult). In the contest I have implied between the two 'foundation myths' of Hungarian history, associated with 15 March and 20 August respectively, solidarity, reconciliation of interests, and a perception of failure are set against division, statesmanship, and power. Hungarian history seems to have shown that you cannot have all of the positive elements of these two combinations together, and the same history inclines more people to prefer the latter to the former. To formulate it in the language of aesthetic theory from my own field, the eighteenth century: 1848 is an unfulfilled love affair with charming beauty, whereas 1000 is the intoxicated admiration of the awesome sublime.

I have deliberately avoided formulating the opposition in terms of liberal–democratic–republican traditions versus monarchism and authority, because not in the least do I want to imply that Hungarians generally prefer authoritarianism to democracy. What I am trying to stress is that there is a discrepancy between the general acceptance of modernity and the transition to democracy on the one hand, and the selection of meaningful traditions on the other. The symbolism of 1848 remains well respected, but it has been overshadowed in public consciousness and in the sweepstakes of official pageantry by one that is more remote and less readily adjusted to the properties of a modern political community at the threshold of the twenty-first century. The myth of Saint Stephen is undoubtedly epochal, and what is even more important from our present perspective, it is not marked by failure; it can even be represented as a triumph over designs against Hungarian sovereignty (a notion that obviously did not exist at the time).

I have claimed that the predominant view of national history in Hungary has for a long time been pathos-ridden and somewhat lacking in a sense of realism and responsibility; I have tried to demonstrate the interplay of these phenomena on the examples of the 'foundation myths' associated with the birth of Hungary as an entity and Hungary as a modern nation; I have endeavoured to relate this to the discriminating attitudes among the public toward these two myths; and I had attempted to explain each of these themes. While I am not suggesting that the priorities between the two should in the future become different (though I think there would be sound reasons in favour of it), this might come about if success and power cease to be the dominant standards against which the merits of traditions are measured, and if other, more inherent values are emphasized in the reflection of history. To finish with Tom Nairn, in the talk quoted at the beginning of this paper he suggested that the restoration of national sovereignty through devolution would create a chance for Scotland to move toward such a situation. The limitations on Hungary's sovereignty were removed a decade ago, but the chance may still not have passed us by.

NOTES

1 László Kontler, *Millennium in Central Europe: A History of Hungary* (Budapest: Atlantisz, 1999). Revised edition as *A History of Hungary: Millennium in Central Europe* (Basingstoke: Palgrave, 2002).

2 Opening address at a conference inaugurating the new Centre for Scottish Studies at Simon Fraser University, Vancouver, Spring 2000.

3 See *Eighteenth-Century Scotland: The Newsletter of the Eighteenth-Century Scottish Studies Society* 14 (Spring 2000): 8.

4 Csaba Csorba, János Estók, and Konrád Salamon, *The Illustrated History of Hungary* (Budapest: Magyar Könyvklub, 1999); originally Gyula Illyés, in *Magyarok* (Budapest, 1938). I owe the reminder of Illyés's words to Nicholas Parsons's review of *The Illustrated History* and my own book in *Hungarian Quarterly* 41 (Summer 2000): 115.

5 Works by outstanding Protestant authors such as András Farkas, Gáspár Károli, and Pál Medgyesi represent this trend, as do arguments by leaders of anti-Habsburg resistance movements such as István Bocskai. See Kálmán Benda, *A magyar nemzeti hivatástudat története (A XVI–XVII. században)* (Budapest, 1937); Sándor Öze, *'Bűneiért bünteti Isten a magyar népet.' Egy bibliai párhuzam vizsgálata a XVI. századi nyomtatott egyházi irodalom alapján* (Budapest: Magyar Nemzeti Múzeum, 1991).

6 Béla Köpeczi, *Magyarország, a kereszténység ellensége* (Budapest: Akadémiai Kiadó, 1977).

7 For a comprehensive treatment, see Larry Wolff, *Inventing Eastern Europe: The Map of Civilization on the Mind of the Enlightenment* (Palo Alto: Stanford University Press, 1994).

8 On Berzeviczy, see Éva H. Balázs, *Berzeviczy Gergely, a reformpolitikus (1763–1795)* (Budapest: Akadémiai, 1967). On the continuity between Enlightenment and the Age of Reform, see the same author's *Hungary and the Habsburgs, 1765–1800: An Experiment in Enlightened Absolutism* (Budapest: Central European University Press, 1997), especially ch. 10; Moritz Csáky, *Von der Aufklärung zum Liberalismus. Studien zur Frühliberalismus in Ungarn* (Vienna: Verlag der Österreichischen Akademie der Wissenschaften, 1981); Charles Kecskeméti, *La Hongrie et le réformisme libéral. Problèmes politiques et sociaux (1790–1848)* (Rome: Centro di ricerca, 1989). For the contrary view, see Domokos Kosáry, *Culture and Society in Eighteenth-Century Hungary* (Budapest: Corvina, 1980).

9 On Széchenyi in English, see George Barany, *Stephen Széchenyi and the Awakening of Hungarian Nationalism, 1791–1841* (Princeton: Princeton University Press, 1968). In Hungarian the best account remains András Gergely, *Széchenyi eszmerendszerének kialakulása* (Budapest: Akadémiai, 1972).

10 Cf. László Péter, 'Volt-e magyar társadalom a XIX. században? A jogrend és a civil társadalom képződése' in *Az Elbától keletre* (Budapest: Osiris, 1998), 148–87.

11 Most recently Domokos Kosáry, *A Görgey-kérdés története*, 2 vols. (Budapest: Osiris, 1996).

12 The two categories overlapped to a considerable extent: the overwhelming majority of the minorities belonged to the peasant population.

13 The authoritative statement of this view was the conservative historian Gyula Szekfü's seminal book *Három nemzedék* (Budapest: Elet, 1920).

14 Erzsébet Andics, 'Kossuth harca az árulók és megalkuvók ellen,' in *Kossuth emlékkönyv* (Budapest: Academiae Scientiarum Hungaricae, 1952); for an analysis of the topic, see László Péter, 'A nemzeti múlt legendái és tilalomfái,' in *Az Elbától keletre*, 96 ff.

15 On the canonization and its ideological significance, see most recently Gábor Klaniczay, *Holy Rulers and Blessed Princesses: Dynastic Cults in Medieval Central Europe* (Cambridge: Cambridge University Press, 2002).

16 For an overview of the literature on the coronation in the postwar period, see Tamás Bogyay's articles in *Új Látóhatár*, 1962 and 1970.

17 *Népszabadság*, 29 December 2000, supplement.

18 Elemér Mályusz, 'Az egynyelvű ország,' *Századok*, 1941.

Cracking Myths of Nation-ness: Indonesia after the Fall of Suharto

BENEDICT ANDERSON

A myth one often encounters is that of each nation's ancient and continuous past: Stonehenge is 'British,' Machu Picchu is 'Peruvian,' the Borobudur is 'Indonesian,' and so on. The myth exists not only at the level of popular folklore, the output of tourist industries, and the state's history textbooks for children and adolescents; one finds it even in the highly sophisticated and erudite work of Professor Anthony Smith, of the London School of Economics, an eminent theoretician of nationalism. His work shows his belief that in the modern era, nations – *real* nations, that is – are built on top of premodern communities of religion, language, homeland, and kin relations, and strengthened by common traditions, values, and symbolic forms.

In thinking about this idea, it is helpful to turn the pages of two kinds of ancient documents, to which in many ways Westerners attribute their common pedigree. First, the Old Testament. Its pages are filled with the names of peoples of whom no trace survives or whose remains are merely archaeological or palaeographic: Assyrians, Amalekites, Canaanites, Babylonians, Edomites, Phoenicians, Moabites, and so forth. No Turks, no Palestinians, no Jordanians, no Saudis. Egyptians, yes – but what today's Egyptians feel they share with the people described in the Old Testament is very far from obvious.

Roman historians described the terrain of today's Turkey as full of Cappadocians, St Paul's Galatians, Bithynians, Cilicians, and even 'Asians' – anything but Turks and Kurds. And, in most cases, we cannot be sure that these peoples were ethnies in the way we understand this word today, because we do not know whether they gave themselves these names or were given them by the imperial ruler. We also do not know whether they were named after places, in the style of British

Columbians and Québécois, or whether they eventually gave their names to their homelands, as the Danes did to Denmark and the Magyars did to Magyarorzag (Hungary).

A look at any reconstructed map of the High Roman Empire reveals that only a tiny minority of the peoples located on it are still familiar to the common reader today: Armenians, Syrians, Egyptians, and a hand-ful of others. Did the huge majority of the empire's peoples fall victim to genocide? Not at all. They migrated, they intermarried, they changed languages and religions, and they joined new economies and civiliza-tions. If they had languages of their own, these died out or combined with other languages, over that long stretch of human history during which illiteracy was the rule and dictionaries and grammars lay in the far future; in other words, in an age when the boundaries between languages were fluid and obscure to everyone. Writing systems, where they existed, very often fell into disuse, and would require immense scientific labour and everyday luck to be deciphered in the nineteenth and twentieth centuries. Such was the norm of human life until quite recently.

One can draw the same lesson even from the exceptional Jews, who are among those peoples who today claim an ancient history. We know that large numbers of Jews stopped being such, vanishing into the Babylonians, Assyrians, Egyptians, and Canaanites over the centuries. The long struggle of the prophets constituted an effort precisely to staunch this continuous hemorrhage. We know too that the languages they spoke changed radically over time and that the spoken national Hebrew of today's Israel has had to be reinvented, out of an old reli-gious language of ritual, in the past eighty years.

The ancient chronicles of Southeast Asia, and the accounts of early European travellers to the region, offer the same general picture. People were casually named by rulers and travellers from relevant toponyms. Balinese were named from the island of Bali, though it is doubtful if any 'Balinese' person thought of herself or himself as such till the twentieth century. The 'Siamese' familiar to French and English travellers and diplomats (and to Khmer and Vietnamese rulers) were an obscure collectivity named after a kingdom. Siam is an old name, which has given us Siamese twins and cats, not Thai twins and cats. The 'Thai' of 'Thailand' are something quite modern.

This pattern has become increasingly normal in the past century. Venezuelans are named after Venezuela, Nigerians after Nigeria, Ku-waitis after Kuwait. It took time and much labour to shift the direction of this causality. On the eve of his execution on the last day of 1896 at the hands of Spanish colonialism, the great Philippine national hero José Rizal wrote a beautiful farewell poem to his *patria adorada* (beloved country), the Philippines – not to his fellow countrymen, because there was as yet no name for these widely differing people. Until his death the word *filipino* meant, in common parlance, only those people of pure Iberian ancestry who happened to be born in the Philippines – that is, local creoles. Beyond them were a huge mass of *indios* ('Indians') and *chinos* ('Chinese'). Today's Filipinos speak of themselves by this term as an ancient people, though the name is derived from a sixteenth-century Spanish king.

Nor was the West terribly different. Jefferson's Declaration of Independence makes no mention of 'Americans.' Fifty years had to pass before Noah Webster published his *Dictionary of the American Language*. The revolution of 1789 was only in retrospect named the 'French' Revolution. Indeed, its enormous international influence derived in part from its being understood as something of universal import, not as something local and Parisian. William Wordsworth, a poet we now think of as terribly English, greeted that revolution with the famous phrase 'Bliss was it in that Dawn to be Alive / And to be Young was Very Heaven.'[1]

This quotation also reminds us that the language of early nationalism was a language of youth, not antiquity. Mazzini's Young Italy and Wolfe Tone's Young Ireland were the forerunners of Burma's Young Men's Buddhist Association, Indonesia's Young Java, and Li Ta-chao's wonderful imagining of 'China in Its Springtime.' These names show, across the globe, what marks nationality off decisively from anything superficially comparable before it: it dreams of the Future – indeed the Future Perfect – here on earth. (No religion believes that nations exist in Heaven or in Hell.) It was, and is, a Common Project. Here we may better understand the modern idea of genocide: the violent, permanent end to a shared Future.

A second myth, which I will address much more briefly and partially, involves the 'hardness' of nations – a hardness that can be viewed from two directions. One might start with space and its strange modern sacralization. In the 1980s, when the debt-ridden American economy seemed to be fading before a triumphant Japan, I used to propose to my students a simple way to solve the colossal American trade deficit. Reminding them that William Seward had bought Alaska from Russia in 1867, I suggested that the time had come to sell it to Japan at a huge profit. Always their jaws fell open. The tradable 'real estate' of 1867 had become off-market 'sacred soil' a century later. America is not exceptional in this regard. All over the world, soil (and offshore water) has become sacred – even if the process of acquisition was European colonial aggression (Africa), imperial administrative division (South America), or dynastic marriage (Europe). The last major redistribution of territories took place in the aftermath of the Second World War in Europe. The USSR broke up along pre-existing political-administrative lines. Most recent examples reveal only Goa and East Timor, perhaps Taiwan in Asia, a near miss in Kuwait, and probably Palestine.

Why this 'hardening' and sacralization? Scientific mapping was always crucial, because it gave each state a continuous (on paper) border, delimited by international law and treaty. This was unlike anything that had existed before. Mapping, combined with exponential expansion of the state's modern functions, created a new idea of sovereignty – one that operated flatly, evenly, and firmly over a mapped space – not the old idea of sovereignty as porous, expandable, and defined by a high centre. And maps eventually turned into logos: every Canadian child will recognize the 'picture' of Canada, even if that picture contains not a single place name.

Language was no less essential. Some languages were being wiped out or relegated to the status of spoken dialects. But others were raised in power and internally consolidated through the vector of print. We can see this clearly from the fact that the English still have (barely) access to Chaucer, but not to the Anglo-Saxon epics. The French can still read Villon, but not the French of the twelfth century. Print drastically slowed down language change. Added to print itself was the impact of grammars and dictionaries, which proliferated in Europe in the eighteenth and nineteenth centuries, showing what was 'Dutch' and not 'German,' what was 'Ukrainian' and not 'Russian.' The imposition of hierarchies on languages was heightened in the nineteenth century through the expansion of huge state-run school systems, which required a 'standard' language for all young to-be citizens.

What the new high language was varied greatly. In the court of the czars, French was spoken until well into the nineteenth century, but the rise of nationalism all over Europe eventually pushed the Romanovs to become more 'national' and Russian-speaking. In the ex-colonial world, however, and above all in Africa and Latin America, the high languages come from Europe: French in Togo and Mali, English in India and Ceylon, Portuguese in Mozambique and Angola, Spanish in Argentina and Colombia. Everywhere, the process was difficult and uneven. Eugen Weber's famous book *Peasants into Frenchmen* discusses the enormous effort made in the later nineteenth century to stop 'Frenchmen' from speaking (or reading) Spanish, Catalan, German, Italian, and Breton, and millions of immigrants from using Polish, Armenian, Arabic, and so forth.

In spite of this 'real' history, nothing is more easily mythologized, and nothing has a more unpredictable fate, than language. Poor José Rizal wrote his great nationalist novels of the Philippines in the late 1880s and early 1890s in what he reverently called the language of Cervantes. But when the Americans seized the Spanish colony in 1898, and built an educational system around American English, Spanish quickly disappeared. Today, young Filipinos have to read the masterworks of their greatest patriot and hero in translation.

I

It is now time to turn specifically to the case of Indonesia and East Timor. All Indonesian history textbooks give the country a history that stretches back to the neolithic period, and none stress the fact that the name 'Indonesia' was invented in the later nineteenth century – and by a German scholar. (We should understand it thus as 'rhyming' with Polynesia, Melanesia, and Micronesia). It did not enter everyday parlance until the 1920s, more than two decades after what is officially regarded as the nationalist movement had gotten under way. The linguistic pioneer was the Indonesian Communist Party. Right up to the Second World War, 'Hindia' – derived from the Dutch East Indies – was also commonly used. Only in the late 1920s did significant numbers of urban, educated natives refer to themselves as 'Indonesians,' but 99 per cent of young Indonesians today are quite unaware of this fact. Astonishing, but quite similar to what one finds in many other parts of the world.

Indonesia's 'sacred territory' was not finally bordered until the 1910s. Most of the gigantic archipelago was only conquered by the Dutch in the second half of the nineteenth century – the bulk of Sumatra, Borneo, Celebes, Papua New Guinea, northern Bali. But in other parts, like Java and Ambon, European rule goes back to the start of the seventeenth century. The boundary between Portuguese East Timor and Dutch West Timor was not settled until a treaty signed in 1915.

Furthermore, under the Japanese Occupation of 1942–5, the Indies were divided into three entirely separate entities: a Sumatra ruled from Singapore and combined with today's West Malaysia; Java; and the so-called Great East. The first two were governed by two separate Japanese armies, the third by the Japanese navy. In the summer of 1945, when the Japanese knew defeat was imminent and still hoped to salvage something from the impending wreckage, they set up a constitutional committee dominated by Indonesian nationalists from all three entities in order to prepare for independence. One major topic of discussion in the committee was national borders. A few firebrands wanted to include ex-British Malaya, all of Borneo, Portuguese East Timor, and so on, on vague grounds of racial brotherhood and linguistic affinity. But wiser heads, aware that the Allies were on their way, prevailed. The committee settled for reunification of the prewar Dutch colony, and in the constitution went out of their way to specify its territorial boundaries, which of course excluded Portuguese East Timor. Over time this constitution became so sacred that it could not be changed, even when the Suharto regime brutally invaded East Timor in 1975. As some ironically minded opposition generals remarked: 'Aside from anything else, the invasion was a massive violation of the Constitution!' This history explains why ordinary Indonesians never felt that the East Timorese were 'really Indonesian,' and why, since East Timor recovered its freedom in 1999, they have ceased to talk or care about it.

Why did Indonesian nationalists quite sincerely decide that the Netherlands East Indies was 'really' Indonesia? The question is especially interesting in that the first generation of nationalists, who were born at the end of the 1880s and in the early 1890s, witnessed as young people the final Dutch conquest of Aceh, West New Guinea, and northern Bali. I believe there were basically three reasons.

First was the (very late) appearance of what I call 'print capitalism' in the Indies. Newspapers owned by Dutchmen only developed in the late 1870s, quickly followed by others owned by Eurasians, Chinese, and eventually natives. All of these newspapers took the Indies as their unselfconscious frame of reference – as the space of 'domestic news' – and their spread in the marketplace disseminated, on an everyday basis, this frame to growing numbers of readers. A European-style school system was established in the 1890s and necessarily had to print thousands of geography and history textbooks for the children it was educating. These students were immediately made acquainted with rectangular Mercatorian maps, dominated by the Indies itself, all one colour, like a jigsaw puzzle piece, with surrounding bits of Malaya, the

Philippines, and East Timor all coloured differently. So the
to grow accustomed to 'seeing' the colony, from God's celes   , ___.. ..
view, as a logoized space. Dutch colonial archaeology framed the country in human time. The marvellous, gigantic Buddhist temple in Central Java called the Borobudur, ignored for centuries by a local population
long since Islamicized, was tidied up and put on display as part of the
colony's ancient heritage. Around 1900 a brilliant French scholar discovered the existence of Srivijaya, a vast maritime empire centred for
five centuries in eastern Sumatra that had been completely forgotten by
the native population. Not surprisingly, the young nationalists seized
on these colonial discoveries to give themselves a splendid and ancient
national history.

And when the children left school, they found themselves living and
working in a space institutionally bounded by the colonialists' ambitions and limitations. Young civil servants could be posted anywhere in
this space, but nowhere outside it. The guilder, or rupiah, circulated
only in the colony, not outside it – and so on.

The second reason was the peculiar linguistic history of the Indies.
This colony was the only one in the world, I think, that was substan-
tially ruled through a non-European language. Very few Indonesians
today are aware of this or of the fact that up to 1940 only a small
percentage of the population used this language on an everyday basis,
and many of these were the much disliked Chinese. But in the past sixty
years it has spread dramatically to the point that it is today the single
most powerful factor cementing Indonesian nationalism. This in turn
helps explain why, when there are large communities of Vietnamese,
Filipinos, and Thais in the advanced countries around the world, comparable communities of Indonesians barely exist. Furthermore, this
language is also the one used to unify the West New Guinean ethnic
groups in their struggle for separation from Indonesia. Its forcible
spread in East Timor after the bloody invasion of 1975 played a role in
the rapid and deepening spread of East Timorese nationalism in the
1990s.

The true origins of what Indonesians today call 'bahasa Indonesia'
are shrouded in nationalist myth, and are of so interesting a character
that some detailed explanation is required. From the start of the seventeenth century, when Dutchmen first settled in the archipelago, up until
the last days of the eighteenth century, what would become Indonesia
was not a true colony, let alone a truly Dutch colony. During those two
centuries, power was in the hands of a private corporation, the United

East India Company, which during its heyday was by far the largest transnational enterprise in the world.

Its commercial and military power stretched from South Africa to the fringes of Japan. Though its board of directors was located in Amsterdam, it employed Germans, Irish, Japanese, Danes, Africans, Malays, 'Indians,' and Swedes as well as Dutchmen. Among the governors general in the archipelago, some of the most able were Protestant French and Germans.

Because it was a profit-making business, the Company saw no reason to waste money on training local people, or even its multiracial, multinational employees, in the Dutch language. It also permitted very little in the way of religious proselytizing: it would have had to pay salaries to missionaries, it feared a backlash from the Muslim peoples it dominated, and Protestant ministers were in short supply even in Holland itself. Nothing offers a sharper contrast than the neighbouring Philippines, where colonization was a project of the Spanish state and the well-manned Catholic Church and the missionary effort was so effective that today the Philippines is overwhelmingly Catholic – the only Christian country in Asia.

What, then, was the Company to do? In the early days it often used Portuguese, which had spread – also through missionaries, merchants, and officials – from India to Formosa during the century before the Dutch arrived in the East. (East Timor fell under Portuguese control in the 1550s, half a century before the Company first made its presence felt in Southeast Asia.) Today there is still a 'Portuguese Church' in Jakarta, so named not because the Portuguese built it – indeed, they never came to Jakarta – but because Portuguese was the *lingua franca* for the city's multicultural, polyglot population. But gradually Portuguese was replaced by a simple pidgin Malay, which had long been used by seafarers and traders across the wide archipelago. Hence when a true Dutch colony was created after the Napoleonic Wars, it inherited a 150-year-old tradition of using pidgin Malay for economic, administrative, and political purposes.

By that time the position of the Dutch language had altered drastically. In Holland's long decline during the eighteenth century, the country's rulers had taken to high-prestige French as their language of social exchange, using Dutch only to deal with domestic servants, peasants, and artisans. By the nineteenth century, Holland had sunk to being a backward, impoverished, and militarily insignificant state. (It had no railways until the 1870s, for example.) French and English were by then 'international languages,' but only three or four million Dutch men and women understood the Dutch language. So even after industrialization began in the 1860s, the Dutch never tried very hard to impose Dutch in the colony – besides, it would have cost far too much money. Today it has virtually disappeared in Indonesia.

For these reasons the colony's rulers picked up where the Company had left off, using what they often referred to as *dienst-maleis* (administrative Malay). Late in the nineteenth century there were efforts to 'clean up' this language through the publication of grammars and dictionaries and through organized borrowings from the High Malay used in the courts of the Malay Peninsula (now in British hands). Within the Indies, the language spread into the market, especially the market of print. Eurasian and Chinese entrepreneurs used it for their newspapers and magazines, and native publishers and journalists quickly followed suit. It became the main language of the schools that finally started to be established in the 1890s in most parts of the huge colony. By 1928 it was ready to be proclaimed as 'our national language' by a Congress of Young Indonesian Nationalists. After all, it was not a European language, it had some speakers in all the main cities, and it was easy to pick up. All that remained was for the young people to forget that they owed most of this to the long-dead Company, and to imagine that they had inherited it from Malay aristocrats along the Straits of Malacca.

Bahasa Indonesia's origins and history gave it singular advantages as a national language. It was not the native language of any important ethnic group in the colony, so everyone could use it as a second language, and no one gained special privileges from it. (One can contrast its political success with the relative failure of Hindi in India, Sinhala in Sri Lanka, and Tagalog in the Philippines – in each of these cases the language belonged to a powerful minority and was widely resented and resisted.) Because it had begun as a pidgin *lingua franca*, it was simple, egalitarian, and easily modernized compared to the notoriously difficult, hierarchical, and feudalized 'regional' languages such as Javanese, Sundanese, and Balinese.

The language's prestige was given a huge and unexpected boost in the 1940s. In 1942, Japanese Emperor Hirohito's armies conquered the Dutch colony in a matter of weeks, soon interned all Dutch people, abolished use of the Dutch language, and systematically promoted Indonesian as the national language. When the Japanese Empire collapsed in August 1945, the Dutch – whose country had been occupied by the Nazis till the previous February – were in no shape to reimpose themselves immediately. Hence an Indonesian Republic was declared and a revolution broke out. By 1946 the Dutch, with help from the British and later the Americans, were taking strong military measures to crush the Republic, but by the end of 1949 they had been forced to transfer sovereignty to their adversaries. During the bitter struggles of 1946–9, millions of Indonesians came to love Bahasa Indonesia as the language of their freedom, of their sacrifices, and of their pride. It had become the language of the anticolonial revolution.

The irony is that under the Suharto dictatorship the language was once again being deployed for – this time brown, not white – colonial purposes. After the invasion of 1975, a great deal of money and violence was deployed in East Timor to wipe out Portuguese and to turn, through the rapidly expanding school system, Timorese children and youths into loyal Indonesians. Yet in the end the language played its own game, by Hegel's 'cunning of reason.' For through their exposure to the Indonesian language, young Timorese obtained linguistic access both to Indonesia and to the outside world. They learned about and from the long-gone Indonesian nationalist movements, and about the once-cherished revolution. They also came to know their enemy very intimately. In the 1910s the dedicated Indonesian nationalist who came to be known as Ki Hadjar Dewantoro published a famous article in Dutch titled 'Als ik eens Nederlander was' (If I were to be, for a moment, a Dutchman), which bitingly attacked the Dutch for their hypocrisy – specifically, for celebrating the anniversary of their own liberation from Napoleon (and forcing the natives to help defray the costs) while depriving Indonesians of their freedom. In the 1990s a young East Timorese militant published, in Indonesian, an article titled 'Seandainya saya seorang Indonesia' (If I were to be, for a moment, an Indonesian'), which excoriated the Suharto regime for doing exactly what the Dutch had done to the Indonesian people.

The third and final reason Indonesian nationalists decided the Netherlands East Indies was the real Indonesia is the imperial imagination itself. We are familiar with the fact that one of the largest and most important provinces of the Roman Empire was called Aegyptus (part of which is today's Egypt). From the high, calm centre in Rome, it was largely a matter of indifference who exactly lived there, even though it was surely understood that the inhabitants spoke many different languages and performed many different religious rituals. They were all 'Egyptians,' named, as it were, after the province. The same style of imagination showed up in the Dutch East Indies. Colonial officials knew very well that they ruled Buddhists, Muslims, Christians, Hindus, and animists and that there were among them dozens of languages, customs, and social systems. But they called them all *inlanders*, which we may translate as 'natives.' Actually, that was the term for natives of this particular colony, because once one travelled to British Malaya, French Indochina, or the Spanish Philippines, one ran into not inlanders but 'natives,' 'indigènes,' and 'indios.' The anthropologically minded census might count Ambonese, Minangkabau, and Sundanese, but colonial law did not. These people were all the same, imagined in the same way as the 'Egyptians' had been. While the low legal status of the inlanders was deeply resented, we can see now that being treated as 'all the same' constituted a powerful base for cross-ethnic and cross-religious solidarity. Hence the inlander is the true ancestor of the Indonesian citizen today – not the Muslim, or the Balinese, or the Christian, or the Menadonese.

The very abjection of the inlander also had unexpected democratizing effects. You could be a Javanese prince, a Buginese nobleman, a Minangakabau ulama, an Ambonese fisherman, or a Sundanese maid – yet you were still 'all the same' before colonialism's racist law. In the end, this levelling produced astonishing opportunities for gifted, unprivileged people who were willing to sacrifice for the national struggle. President Sukarno was the son of a Javanese schoolteacher and a Balinese woman. Vice-President Hatta was born into a low-level official's family in West Sumatra. All the impressive leaders of the nationalist movement, who are today regarded as national heroes, were ex-inlanders.

The irony is that these processes were later recapitulated after Indonesia gained its independence. The cases of West New Guinea and East Timor are exemplary. In the vast, underpopulated, and isolated space of West New Guinea, there were (and are) about two hundred ethnolinguistic groups, often traditional enemies of one another, and usually speaking mutually unintelligible languages. This wild array was inassimilable by the distant national capital and its elites. So Sukarno invented an 'Egyptian' name for the place and the imagined homogeneous collectivity of its people: Irian – an acronym derived from the words Ikut Republik Indonesia Anti-Nederland, meaning Joining the Republic of Indonesia and Against the Netherlands – had of course its 'Irianese.' The name was immediately and widely accepted by Indonesian society; not only that, but it also became the quasi-legal basis for homogenizing administrative practices and (often oppressed) political status. In the time of Portuguese colonialism, 'East Timor' contained at least twenty distinct linguistic groups; while some of these languages were related to the Melanesian family, others belonged to the utterly different Austronesian family (to which most Indonesian languages belong). But in the eyes of Lisbon, which could not have cared less about the Atoni, the Mambe, and so on, they were all 'East Timorese,' even if they could not understand one another and often did not like one another other much. After the 1975 invasion, Jakarta picked up where Lisbon left off. It regarded these people as 'East Timorese' and violently treated them as such – long before most of them regarded themselves this way. By the same processes through which 'Indonesians' were born out of inlanders, so out of 'administrative East Timorese' and 'bureaucratic Irianese' were born the self-aware patriots who call themselves the East Timorese Nation, and the Organisasi Papua Merdeka, or Organization for a Free Papua. However, one should be aware that these imagined communities do not include West Timor or Papua-Niugini.

Today these constitute powerful nationalist identities, even though they did not seriously exist thirty-five years ago. Yet already we can observe the same process of forgetting that is characteristic of all modern nationalisms. Just as Indonesians no longer remember that in part they owe their wonderful national language to the hated United East India Company, and their glorious past to Dutch archaeologists and a French epigrapher, so Papuan nationalists (who use Indonesian as their *lingua franca*) and East Timorese patriots are forgetting that the imaginings and practices of their colonial oppressors made important if unconscious contributions to their novel solidarity. Today, both Papuans and East Timorese are busy imagining their antiquity, not their novelty. 'They' have 'always been there.'

At the same time, one must never forget the real peculiarity of nationalism, which I mentioned at the start of this essay. It imagines polities that are unique in world history in that they have the future as their compass, and a future not in heaven but here on earth. In this way, it thinks about 'where we are heading' as much as 'where we came from.' This future is not exactly a myth, though it has definite and agreeable millenarian overtones. It is a future that we share with Indonesians and East Timorese, whether we are Canadians, Slovenians, Angolans, or Peruvians. This future encourages us to make sacrifices of time, money, and personal pleasure for the millions of national unborn we will never live to see. For them, we worry about national nature reserves, and about the environment. We pay taxes in long-term public investments of a hundred kinds – schools, universities, museums, highways, and so on – out of which we, as mortal individuals, will perhaps receive only minor and fleeting benefits. And we are able to feel ashamed of our nation's bad behaviour and the sometimes criminal practices of our nation's rulers, exactly because we have a future to which we feel accountable. It was this shame that drove frail and elderly Americans into the streets to protest against the savage idiocy of the American state's onslaught in Indochina. It is the same shame that drives comfortably-off Indonesian lawyers to devote themselves to helping the victims of the Indonesian military's brutal rapacity. They want a better future for their country. Don't we all?

NOTES

1 William Wordsworth, *The Fourteen-Book Prelude*, edited by W.J.B. Owen (Ithaca: Cornell University Press, 1985).

Contributors

Benedict Anderson is a professor of government at Cornell University. Apart from being a renowned specialist on Southeast Asia, he is the author of the widely discussed *Imagined Communities: Reflections on the Origin and Spread of Nationalism* (1983, revised edition 1991) and *The Spectre of Comparison: Nationalism Southeast Asia and the World* (1998).

Ramsay Cook is Professor Emeritus of History at York University and general editor of the *Dictionary of Canadian Biography/Dictionnaire biographique du Canada*. His publications include *Canada, Quebec and the Uses of Nationalism* (1986) and *The Maple Leaf Forever: Essays on Nationalism and Politics in Canada* (1971).

Thomas Ferenczi is a senior editor of the French daily *Le Monde*, where he has worked in various capacities since 1971. He has been a visiting professor at Yale University. His publications include *D'une France a l'autre* (1974), *Chronique du septennat* (1988), and *Figures de l'événement* (2000).

Sima Godfrey is director of the Institute for European Studies at the University of British Columbia, where she also teaches French literature in the Department of French, Italian, and Hispanic Studies. Her work has focused largely on nineteenth-century French literature and cultural history. She is currently working on a book on the concept of fashionability in modern French culture.

Andreas Heinemann-Grüder is a senior researcher at the Bonn International Centre for Conversion, specializing on post-Soviet and Eastern

European Politics. He teaches comparative politics at Cologne University. Former affiliations include the Free University of Berlin, Humboldt University Berlin, and the University of Pennsylvania.

László Kontler is professor and head of the history department at Central European University in Budapest. His research and publications focus on early-modern European intellectual history. His most recent publication is *A History of Hungary: Millennium in Central Europe* (2002).

Marta Petrusewicz emigrated from her native Poland in 1969 and has since lived in Italy, Canada, and the United States. She has taught at the Universita della Calabria, Harvard, Princeton, and currently at the City University of New York. She has published extensively on the economic and social history of Italy and Poland and is now at work on a comparative history of the nineteenth-century European peripheries.

Dietmar Schirmer is DAAD-Professor of Government at Cornell University. He earned his PhD at the Free University of Berlin and works in the fields of European social systems, state formation in Europe, comparative nationalism, political aesthetics, and political culture. Recent publications include *Identity and Intolerance* (co-edited with Norbert Finzsch, 1998), and *Politik und Bedeutung* (co-edited with Werner Rossade and Birgit Sauer, 2002).

Frank Unger is professor at the Institute for European Studies at the University of British Columbia. He taught at the Free University of Berlin and at Humboldt University Berlin and was a visiting professor at Oregon State University's Center for the Humanities. His research fields are European-U.S. relations, international political economy, and the contemporary history of Europe and Germany. His book publications include *Amerikanische Mythen* (1988) and *Amerika – Der gespaltene Traum* (with L. Carlson, 1992).